Best Wishes

Frank Beer.

'THE ANGEL OF LOVE'

Emily Hobhouse, 1860 - 1926

First published 2002
Copyright © 2002 Frank H. Beer
B.Ed. C.N.A.A. Cert. Ed. Cert. R. Ed.

Author - Frank H. Beer

Books available from,

CHARATON BOOKS
HIGHER CHARATON
GOLBERDON ROAD
PENSILVA
LISKEARD
CORNWALL
PL14 5RW
UNITED KINGDOM
FAX/PHONE 01579/363280

Printed in Great Britain by
Polpentre Design & Print,
Tredinnick, Duloe,
Cornwall,
United Kingdom.

I.S.B.N. Number 0-9543364-0-2 THE ANGEL OF LOVE

CONTENTS

	Introduction	7
1.	The Heyday of Imperialism	9
2.	The Hobhouse family in St Ive, Cornwall	13
3.	A New Life	19
4.	War Inevitable	33
5.	The Political Scene	41
6.	Farm Burning	49
7.	Shouted Down	55
8.	A Visit to The South African Camps	77
9.	Return to the UK	103
10.	The Committee Of Lady Visitors	117
11.	Deported	129
12.	The Prisoner Returns	139
13.	The Suffering Of The Blacks	143
14.	Peace in South Africa	149
15.	Dear Mr Gandhi	161
16.	World War One	167
17.	The Aftermath Of War	177
18.	Physical Deterioration	181
19.	The Influence Of The Times	187
	Epilogue	191
	Appendices	195
	Bibliography	209

EMILY HOBHOUSE, 1901

Every Society needs characters of a
Noble Spirit
Without them no Society can look forward
to Progress (anon)

FOREWORD

Emily Hobhouse, 1860 - 1926, known as The Angel Of Love, was a whistleblower who drew international attention to the suffering that Britain facilitated in the concentration camps it set up in South Africa during the Boer War.

As a result, she was vilified in her own country but honoured by ordinary South Africans to the extent that she became known as The Angel Of Love and had her remains interred at the national memorial in Bloemfontein, where only presidents had previously been buried.

Because of that affection for her in South Africa, she appeared on a South African postage stamp in 1976.

In Britain she is virtually unknown, but in South Africa she remains a heroine.

Emily Hobhouse was born in the village of St Ive,. near Liskeard in Cornwall on 9th April 1860. This book entitled The Angel Of Love is a tribute to her and is the result of a five year labour of love. I myself am a Plymothian, who was born nearby, at Stonehouse, Devon. I wish to bring Emily the posthumous recognition that she so justly deserves.

Frank H. Beer

Acknowledgments

I appreciate the generous encouragement given to me, whilst formulating this tribute to Emily Hobhouse, by the following;

Firstly my family and in particular my wife Beryl;

The Rev Ron Lucas;

Jennifer Hobhouse Balme, Great Niece of Emily Hobhouse.

Trevor Richards - General Manager, The Porthminster Hotel, St Ives, Cornwall;

Mike Aaronson - General Secretary, Save the Children;

Mr & Mrs B. Gardner - Harewood House, Calstock, Cornwall;

Sir John and Lady Trelawny;

Jon Massey - who assisted in the editing of this book;

and finally,

The Right Hon. Tony Wedgewood Benn MP.
(whose father was also a humanitarian pioneer)

Frank H. Beer

INTRODUCTION

EMILY Hobhouse came from a genteel, upper-class background. Her father, Reginald, was the Rector of St Ive Parish Church in East Cornwall and was the product of a well-known aristocratic family. His wife, Caroline Trelawny, was a descendant of Bishop John Trelawny, immortalised in the Cornish anthem And Shall Trelawny Die?

Emily rose to prominence during the Boer War, when British troops embarked on a system of farm burning and placing women and children into concentration camps. Many innocent people died through disease, malnutrition and general neglect.

Emily went to South Africa and visited the camps, organising help, and she revealed the truth about the terrible camp conditions to the British nation.

Her denunciation of the war, and her humanitarian nature, resulted in Emily being referred to by the jingoistic British public as a Pro-Boer.

In contrast, she became known in South Africa as The Angel Of Love.

In 1919, she helped starving children in Leipzig, Germany, with the assistance of Save The Children and her own funds, and she gave aid to starving Russian mothers and babies during the Russian Revolution.

She also found time to be heavily involved in the campaigns for votes for both men and women. Her positive and public addresses helped pave the way for female emancipation – in many ways epitomising the slogan of the Suffragettes, "Deeds not words".

Emily Hobhouse abhorred hatred and violence, and was even approached by Mahatma Gandhi for help in his quest for recognition for the South African Indian minority.

After Emily's death in 1926, her ashes were interred at the National Memorial in Bloemfontein, South Africa, an honour equivalent to being laid to rest in Westminster Abbey.

— FRANK H BEER
B.Ed. C.N.A.A. Cert. Ed. Cert. R. Ed.

THE HEYDAY OF IMPERIALISM

T HE SUN that was supposed never to set on the British Empire began to do so shortly before the death of Queen Victoria. The British Empire, a self-satisfied colossus of influence and power, embarked upon a military campaign in October 1899 against the Boers in South Africa.

It was expected to be an easy victory for the British – but initially, it went very badly against them, with a devastating effect on national feelings and pride.

No-one could have been more surprised than the Queen, who had decreed, in a privately-uttered statement: "We are not interested in the possibilities of defeat – they do not exist."

It was the supreme example of a positive, almost dogmatic attitude that was felt with pride, by many British nationals, mainly at home in Britain.

Jingoism, belligerent foreign policy, and a total lack of self-criticism, were almost de rigueur as a national attitude.

The minority, who were apprehensive about supporting a potential head-on conflict with the Boers, were referred to as Pro-Boers.

Even young British children were drawn into the maelstrom of national superiority and pride which lasted well into the 20th Century, as the following verse of a well-known song of the period illustrates: "We are the children of the Empire / The greatest nation on the Earth / Loyal children we / Happy gay and free / Claiming Britain for our birth."

As the war progressed, those lyrics were to represent the opposite of what the Boer children, and many of their mothers, were experiencing.

Rudyard Kipling stoked the fires of jingoism with poems and stories revealing the admirable qualities of the common British soldier, while the music halls echoed his genius for prose in musical form, unleashing even more patriotic fervour.

At the final curtain, the audience would stand, many at rigid attention, while the National Anthem was played as a loyal gesture (a tradition that persisted in British cinemas well into the 1960s).

Even on the high seas around the globe, all ships, when passing a Royal Navy man-o-war, would lower their flags as a mark of respect to the Imperial White Ensign. This was looked upon by many British nationals as a sign of the superiority of the British navy and nation.

Newspapers even carried adverts reflecting this zealous national attitude. One example, in The Cornish Times of Saturday 30 June 1900, entreated readers thus: "Three Cheers for the Queen, Three Cheers for Lord Roberts, Three Cheers for the Yarmouth Clothing Company."

Field Marshal Lord Roberts, VC, was the Commander-In-Chief of the British Army in South Africa.

The late Victorian age was in many ways a society to

which it was a privilege to belong – depending, of course, on your place in it. The impact of Darwinism on the Bible's version of Man's origins heralded an age of enlightenment.

The new Education Act turned education into a vehicle by which people could rise through the social class system.

The age of mass production through machinery and mechanical expertise; a new mobility via railways, trams, buses, steam ships and bicycles; overseas trade improvements, facilitating port development and increased employment; faster communication, using the new telegraph system; photography, which could convey positive or negative propaganda… all of these things made Victorians feel they were at the hub of the world.

But on their own doorsteps, the Salvation Army aroused attention in their efforts to help the poor and needy, the homeless and social outcasts. Thanks to them, debtors and harlots and people suffering from the evils of drink were given spiritual guidance and sustenance. Temperance and sobriety movements, coupled with the new restrictions and regulations on gin palace and pub opening hours, contributed to worthwhile living.

Reading, music, card and game playing, trips to the seaside, or for big town shopping, all contributed to a better quality of life. It is little wonder that so many members of society enthusiastically supported the highly successful regime of national pride, with an Empire so superbly protected by the Imperial Army and Royal Navy, that brooked no interference whatsoever.

Then along came Emily Hobhouse.

THE RECTORY AT ST. IVE, EAST CORNWALL

Now a private residence.
Emily lived there in her earlier years, 1860-1895

The Hobhouse Family In St Ive, Cornwall

<hr>

S T IVE, pronounced phonetically "Saint Eve" and not to be confused with St Ives (as in ivy), is on the East of the Cornish peninsula, between Callington and Liskeard. To the west in a valley is the old manor house of Trebeigh, a quarter of a mile from the church.

In the year 1150, during the Christian Crusade period, it is recorded that the Lordship of the Manor of Trebeigh was presented by King Stephen to the Knights Templars, an extremely powerful organisation of Cistercian monks who gave hospitality and sustenance to any pilgrims to the Holy Land.

The tithes of the Knights Templars of St Ive Parish Church were held from 1150 to 1312.

Emily's father, the Reverend Reginald Hobhouse, was Rector of St Ive Parish Church from 1844 until his death in 1895 and he was also Archdeacon of Bodmin.

But he was not St Ive's most famous incumbent. That title went to the Reverend John Trelawny, who, in 1677, also held the livings of South Hill and Callington. He was later to be appointed Bishop of Bristol in 1685.

In April 1688, King James II ordered the Bishops to have The Declaration Of Indulgence read in all churches.

The Archbishop of Canterbury and six other Bishops, including Bishop John Trelawny, refused to comply with the King's order.

They were all imprisoned in the Tower of London, accused of seditious libel, but a public outcry on their behalf led to their eventual acquittal.

The Cornish, in particular, were ready to march on London, inspired by the song that is still on every true Cornishman's lips today: "And shall Trelawny die? / Then twenty thousand Cornishmen / shall know the reason why."

Reginald Hobhouse's father, whose family came from Somerset, was Permanent Under Secretary at the Home Office, to Sir Robert Peel, then Prime Minister, who made Reginald Rector of St Ive.

On Wednesday 13 August, 1851, Reginald married Caroline Trelawny. She was the daughter of Sir William Lewis Salusbury Trelawny, descended from Sir Jonathan Trelawny, 1556-1604. Caroline spent her childhood at the family home, Harewood, in Calstock.

Reginald installed his young bride in a newly-constructed rectory, opposite the church in St Ive, that had been designed especially for Caroline, with very roomy accommodation for a future family and guests.

Reginald and Caroline had eight children. The first and second child died at an early age. The surviving children, in order of descendency, were Caroline, 1854, Alfred, 1856, Blanche, 1857, Maude, 1858, Emily, 9 April 1860, and Leonard, 1864.

Caroline had a household staff, freeing her to concentrate on giving her children a happy and informative childhood, and Reginald was able to devote his life and energy to parish affairs.

The family led a happy, cohesive life, with the usual pets, short trips to the beautiful surrounding countryside, occasional holidays at the seaside, and shopping trips by pony and trap to nearby Callington and Liskeard.

On one such family holiday to the South of France, the family lost Blanche, who died in Toulouse in May 1877 at the age of 19.

Three years after the tragedy, Emily's mother, Caroline, died of a brain tumour.

Reginald, in the meantime, was committed to travelling away from the parish due to his extra duties and functions as Archdeacon of Bodmin.

Emily's elder sister, Caroline, having married away from home in 1876, left Maude and Emily to undertake the household responsibilities, including caring for the Archdeacon.

In 1889, Maude married one of the local curates, Ernest Hebblethwaite, contrary to her father's wishes, and they moved away to North Cornwall, settling into a smaller parish.

That left Emily alone to cope with caring for her ageing father, whose health was gradually deteriorating.

Although in later years Emily observed that she had not received a formal education, she had, in fact, developed considerable talents.

She enjoyed painting plants and flowers, having had tuition in Liskeard, she studied and practised the violin and singing, and in 1876 joined her sister Maude at a finishing school in London.

On her return to St Ive, Emily's interests gradually developed into parochial involvements, exploiting her talents, such as leading the singing, playing the organ, and helping to instruct the younger children attending Sunday School.

She also assisted in parish youth work and organisation and visited the sick and elderly on behalf of her father. She also undertook general social responsibilities, giving assistance and advice to people suffering from minor ailments.

This was of great necessity as the local doctor lived many miles away. Visiting destitute families, of which there were several in the parish, was yet another area of Emily's concern and involvement.

Emily was also helpful in opening and supporting a reading room-cum-library in Pensilva. It was especially appreciated by the local youth of the village.

To mark his 50 years in the post, Reginald was presented with an illuminated testimonial and a silver tray, as a token of the esteem held for him as "a gentleman with tact, total integrity, impeccable fatherly counselling and brotherly advice, in time of need".

As her father drifted towards his death, Emily had begun reading newspapers to him, including The Times.

It followed that her own awareness of and personal insight into local, national and worldwide events, and concerns, became extensive.

Her many discussions with her father and Leonard, her liberal-minded brother, must have brought out an independent and decisive streak in Emily's caring character.

Just prior to her final departure from the Rectory, after the death of her father, Emily received a letter from the local Friendly Society.

The letter of appreciation for her good work was also deeply thankful for her dedication and for the many memorable hours spent by local youths at the reading centre.

The following is a report of her father's will in The Cornish Times:

The Will of the late Ven Reginald Hobhouse, Rector of St Ive, Cornwall, formerly Archdeacon of Bodmin, who died on 27 January, was proved on 25 February by Rev F T Batchelor and Leonard Trelawny Hobhouse (Son), two of the Executors, the value of the personal Estate amounting to £32,904.

The Testator gives £100 to the South Devon and East Cornwall Hospital; £200 towards the erection of a Mission Chapel or Chapel of Ease at Pensilva; a quarter's rent to each of his tenants on the glebe; such sum as will provide double pay for each pauper in the parish for one week; a like sum to be given away in blankets, cotton sheets, and coals to poor labouring people who are not paupers, and many other legacies. As to the residue of his property, he leaves one fifth to each of his children, Leonard Trelawny, Alfred Henry, Maud and Emily; and one fifth to his son-in-law, Augustus Vansittart Thornton.

It can be assumed that each of his children, plus one son-in-law, would have received a sum in the region of £6,000, a large amount of money at the time.

Emily Hobhouse. 1895.

In mourning attire, to respect the memory of death of Father "Reginald".

A New Life

————⟫•◦•⟪————

IN CONSIDERING her future role in life, Emily went temporarily to stay with her brother Leonard in Oxford, where he was engaged in tutorials at his old college, Corpus Christi. She was very close to Leonard, whose philosophical outlook in politics and the social order stimulated Emily and might have been at least partly responsible for her liberal disposition.

Leonard was a brilliant academic with a photographic memory, a master at the art of intellectual discussion, and a dynamic philosopher.

After attending Marlborough College, he gained a scholarship, and went to Corpus Christi College, Oxford, where, in 1890, he took up an appointment as an assistant tutor and four years later was elected a Fellow.

In 1897, Leonard joined The Manchester Guardian newspaper. Its editor, C P Scott, had been aware of Leonard's great talents and Leonard, at that stage, preferred a change from lecturing on sociological subjects.

He was an emotional person, with a remarkable memory, a basic sense of humour, and a fluent conversationalist.

In becoming a Professor of Sociology at London University, Leonard published many philosophical and political books.

Having a strong interest in trade unionism, he wrote The Labour Movement, published in 1893; The Theory Of Knowledge, 1896; Mind In Evolution, 1901; and many other social and philosophic publications.

Both he and Emily were members of the Adult Suffrage Society.

At that time, Women's Suffrage was gaining momentum as an important social issue.

In order to gain a foothold, some mainly middle-class women thought it prudent to pursue the course of a limited franchise, by restricting their cause purely to privileged members of the middle- and upper-class.

The Adult Suffrage Society were against this; their truly democratic aim was to work toward suffrage for all members of society of adult age.

Opinion and awareness of women's rights were being highlighted elsewhere as the following chronological table depicts:

9 March 1900 – Germany:
Women petition the Reichstag for the right to sit state examinations and to attend university.

8 April 1901 – Belgium:
Social Democratic Conference adopts policy of universal suffrage.

21 December 1901 – Norway:
Women vote for the first time, but only in local elections.

29 December 1901 – United Kingdom:
Woman House Surgeon in Macclesfield is forced to resign because male colleagues refuse to work with her in view of her sex.

1 February 1902 – China:
Imperial decree abolishes binding of women's feet and ends the ban on mixed marriages.

18 February 1902 – London:
37,000-signature petition is presented to Parliament by women textile workers, demanding votes for women.

Sadly, it was not until the end of the 1914-18 war that women in the United Kingdom were granted the freedom to vote.

In the 1850s, secondary education for girls in Great Britain and other European countries was very ill-provided-for. They were sacrificed to pay for the expensive education of their brothers.

In that, and other matters concerning women, emancipation and improvement was postponed.

Awareness of female social conditions encouraged Emily to participate in the struggle taking place in Victorian society towards emancipation for women.

Being part Cornish, the Celtic side of her inheritance spared her from having a totally English outlook, and she identified instead with the Irish, Scots and the Welsh.

She was a loving, strong-willed, independent woman with a highly intellectual and forgiving Christian nature.

The Cornish desire for independence is strongly felt in current times with the movement Mebyon Kernow ("Sons of Cornwall") leading the revival of the Cornish language, and the Gorsedd Council, to which being selected as a Bard of Cornwall is a rare and prestigious honour.

And a political movement for Cornish independence is still very much alive.

One of Emily's favourite walks was to the village of Pensilva about two miles to the north west. In walking there, by way of the general direction of Trebeigh, Emily used to pass a farmstead very near to the village.

One of the occupants was William John Barrett. Emily, in her late twenties, struck up a relationship with him.

It was common knowledge throughout the village that a fairly serious romance was under way between Emily and the farmer's son. News of the relationship got back to St Ive and Emily's father, the Reverend Hobhouse who, for reasons of his own, disapproved and broke up the relationship between Emily and her boyfriend.

Barrett temporarily emigrated to America, and returned a reasonably wealthy man but never again entered into any relationship with Emily.

It may well be that the aristocratic but determinedly academic cleric disliked the idea of his daughter Emily becoming a hardworking farmer's wife.

Emily's chances of finding a suitable husband were limited in the local community. Although festooned with various mine workings, there was a paucity of eligible men. This was mainly due to the mines becoming unviable with many young men leaving the district.

Many other developing areas in the world were demanding the much-praised skills of the Cornish miner. Fame, fortune and adventure awaited those willing to boldly seek a new way of life.

In mid 1895, Emily left for the United States, with the intention of working socially for the good of mankind.

She planned to help in the welfare of the many Cornish miners who had gone to the Minnesota area.

Because of their great expertise and experience in deep mining, Cornish miners were very much sought-after in the developing United States.

In St Paul, Minnesota, Emily immersed herself in church work in the remote mining town of Virginia.

A pioneer town, founded in 1892, it was a typical Wild West town with wide streets, wooden houses and shacks, and wooden sidewalks.

The town also had more than 40 saloon bars, minimal sanitation, speakeasies, and many females, some of easy virtue.

Emily had entered a corrupt and hard-drinking, gambling society.

Her main occupation involved the promotion of temperance, in an effort to combat the severe social drinking habits suffered, or enjoyed, by the 4,000 miners who ranged around the town.

With her usual devotion, she organised a church choir, a

Sunday School, and a library, raising funds locally for the project.

Having witnessed the happy marriages of her brothers and sisters, and being trusting and loving herself, it is little wonder that Emily wanted to get married.

Emily made the acquaintance of John Carr Jackson, a general store owner who was involved in political and social circles.

Many people had been assisted by Jackson's help and advice and it appeared that JCJ, as he would have been known, hankered after a seat in the US Congress.

Emily, a refined, vivacious, attractive woman who was obviously of independent means, became a target for Jackson's advances. And she fell for Jackson's good looks and articulate, humorous ways.

As time progressed, there also developed a series of differences of opinions, which blew hot and cold between them.

Emily had fallen in love, but had mixed emotions about the man.

As her time in Minnesota had almost expired, Emily returned to Britain for a short while, partially to discuss things with her family and to assess her own feelings away from the presence of Jackson.

It is obvious that despite all the arguments with Jackson, she was still very much attracted to him, as she eventually returned to the Minnesota area.

During Emily's absence, Jackson had become Mayor of the town of Virginia.

This time, the more Emily saw of Jackson, the more obsessed she became with him.

In July 1896, she finally promised her hand to Jackson, and they began to plan for a future together.

But Virginia began to suffer the stresses of a depression and two of the largest US mining companies, Carnegie and Rockerfeller, were engaged in a financial conflict.

Local mines, timber mills and businesses were folding up rapidly every day.

Jackson's business interests and his trading store fell into deep trouble.

He had parted with goods on credit and trust, and when his debtors couldn't pay up, he began to suffer severe financial difficulties.

When his mayoralty came to an end, the couple decided to leave Virginia and move to Mexico.

History records that Jackson left town in a hurry, after selling off his business. He was said to have left behind a mass of legal and financial complications.

Having promised to join Emily later, he left her to travel on to Mexico on her own.

On her arrival (and whether it was on Jackson's advice, it is not clear) Emily was advised to invest some of her money in a ranch in Mexico.

It had been claimed that this particular ranch was prolific in the production of coffee, with banana plantations and pineapple fields.

But it turned out that the ranch was in such a remote area that Emily, being on her own, could not bring herself to visit it. Although she told her brother, Leonard, that it was a good, lucrative investment, it became obvious that it was a miserable failure.

Emily was devastated and upset, feeling she had been deceived. She lost £1,200 – a huge amount of money in those days.

And still she waited in vain for Jackson to join her in Mexico City.

In the following Spring, Emily returned to the United States, and once again had a short reunion with Jackson in Chicago.

He was still on the verge of bankruptcy, and had been ordered by a court to answer allegations levelled by several organisations and companies.

It is not clear whether he became a fugitive from justice, but the intended marriage to Emily never took place.

In the meantime, Emily, a broken-hearted, harshly-treated woman, returned almost penniless to Britain, stating that she would wait for Jackson for "as long as it takes".

On returning to the United Kingdom, Emily settled into a flat in Chelsea and made friends with Kate Courtney, wife of Leonard Courtney, a Liberal MP.

Emily soon became involved in writing, mainly social reports, and most of them about the socially disadvantaged.

In one such report of more than 5,000 words, and largely documented, she described the unsocial conditions female London Dockland workers were experiencing in clearing garbage.

Emily kept up a regular communication with her brother

Leonard on the Manchester Guardian, a Liberal newspaper.

Both he and Emily were keen members of the Liberal Movement and, like many fellow members, were strongly against the imminent South African Boer War.

In the Spring of 1899, Sir Alfred Milner, in South Africa, alleged in a telegram home to Parliament that there were thousands of Uitlanders under the yoke of the Boers, and were virtually slaves.

This provocative message led to the British meeting the Boers at the Free State capital for the Bloemfontein Conference on 31 May 1899.

The meeting failed to resolve outstanding differences and both sides prepared to mobilise for war.

At this stage, we should recall the circumstances leading up to the impasse at the Bloemfontein Conference.

The Dutch were the first Europeans to settle in the South African Cape area.

In 1652, a port-of-call was established as an intermediate station for Dutch ships plying between Holland and the Dutch East Indies.

From 1685, several hundred Huguenots who had fled to Holland began, with Dutch assent, to colonise the Cape.

The Huguenots had originally fled to Holland from France, after being persecuted following Louis XIV's revocation of the Edict of Nantes.

As time progressed, the Huguenots and the Dutch settlers at the Cape inter-married. Making their livelihood mainly from farming, the settlers were described as Boers, a Dutch word for farmers. They were spread over a wide area, in a male dominated society. Each family was autonomous, although in serious situations, they co-operated closely.

Because many of them knew only too well about drastic religious persecution, they were almost fanatic in adhering to their own faith.

They thought themselves superior to others, especially the indigenous black population, treating them virtually as slaves.

Although slavery was by then an unacceptable concept to the British, both Britain and America had previously condoned black subservience when it suited their own purposes.

Slavery had been abolished by Act of Parliament throughout the British Empire in 1833 and President Lincoln had proclaimed the abolition of slavery in the United States of America in 1863.

It should also be recalled that, prior to the Factory Acts of 1833-47, young children in working-class families were being exploited in Britain.

The average age at which children were employed in the factories was eight, and the working day, in some cases, extended to 18 hours.

As late as 1844, an Act was passed, limiting female workers to 12 hours per day, and eight to 13-year-olds to six-and-a-half hours daily.

There were no recognised paid holidays, and a six-day week was the norm.

Even seamen, on Royal Naval Ships on anti-slavery patrols, were subject to authoritarian suppression and it was not until 1880 that flogging was abolished.

The anti-slavery movement, well established in Britain, began to gather momentum in the Cape colony.

The London Missionary Society were engaged in Christian conversion, baptism and freeing people from slavery.

This upset many Boer farmers, turning them against the London Missionary Society, the Crown Commissioners, and the British generally.

The cheap labour provided by the indigenous population was diminishing severely.

So, towards the mid 1800s, the Boers began an exodus from the area to show their rejection of the policy of equality for blacks and whites.

Separating themselves from officialdom, the Boers considered themselves free from British restraints.

But the missionaries, through the London Missionary Society, attempted to influence the British authorities to extend their influence into the newly-settled areas.

They did not succeed, and in 1852 the British Government recognised the independence of the Orange Free State and the Transvaal.

This led to further trouble. In 1866, gold was discovered in the Rand in the heart of the Transvaal which brought about a rush of prospecting and mining immigrants.

It has been estimated that during the period 1875-1911, the European-descended population grew from 328,000 to

I,276,000. These people, known as Uitlanders, brought with them many social problems, including gambling, and hard drinking.

The liquor laws and restrictions of sale, as administered by the Boer Authorities, were very lax.

One of the primary concessions adopted by the Boers in 1881 was a liquor monopoly.

Near Pretoria, there was an establishment with the sole right to distil liquor. The prosperous business was based mainly on sales to the indigenous workers, with few or no restrictions.

Many of them were, as a result, perpetually inebriated. Fights and riots were common among the mine workers, causing terrible social and employment problems. And company managers estimated a 25 per cent loss in labour and production fees.

The Chamber Of Mines made frequent protests about the liquor problem, without serious effect. And this was not helped by claims that the police were in league with the liquor barons.

These and many other social ills were reprehensible to the Bible-orientated Boer settlers. Being generally very perturbed over further interference, many more Boers, known as Voertrekkers, moved on, but some with local interests remained.

Those who moved were a tough, versatile and resilient society, challenging the hostility of not only the Veldt, but the indigenous population themselves.

They crossed the mainly hostile terrain with their own

provisions and cooking utensils, relying on locally-obtained firewood for cooking.

With a very impressive knowledge of herbal remedies to cure their ills, the Boers had no medical resources to rely upon and certainly no doctors or midwives to aid them.

If the senior male was ill, or injured, the females were more than capable of driving wagons up and down the often steep terrain.

In the absence of teachers, both parents taught their own children hunting, marksmanship, reading and general studies, including the scriptures.

They were a healthy breed, with a strong sense of cleanliness, discarding rubbish and excreta in a proper manner, and always camping downstream of any fresh water supply.

When attacked, they would form a protective ring or laager with their wagons.

Resisting attack from within the circle, they were excellent marksmen, while their wives and older children were formidable foes to encounter.

In 1871, diamonds were discovered at Kimberley, which gave rise to a further influx of Uitlanders after riches.

Resentment toward the Boers was heightened when they began to tax the prospecting immigrants very heavily.

The Uitlanders were also denied all political rights and representation.

This was despite their owning a large proportion of the land in the Transvaal and approximately 90% of the wealth.

The situation reached fever pitch when the Uitlanders

undertook a very emotional anti-Boer campaign, backed by the slogan "No taxation without representation".

In an effort to kindle an insurrection against the Boers, a futile and wholly discreditable raid into the Transvaal took place in 1895. It was led by Dr L S Jameson, a close friend of Cecil Rhodes, who had a massive pecuniary interest and influence in the diamond industry.

The "Jameson Raid" proved an absolute failure, but triggered an anti-British reaction by President Kruger of the Transvaal, and his associates, who successfully suppressed the raid.

German sympathy for the Boers was evident when it became known that the German Emperor had sent a telegram of congratulations to the Boer president over the suppression of the raid.

The British Government's reaction to the situation, influenced by the attitudes of the Colonial Secretary, Joseph Chamberlain, Lord Milner, British High Commissioner for the Cape, and Cecil Rhodes, made war inevitable.

Chamberlain, backed by Britain's military might, was certainly not afraid of a political dispute.

Rhodes, a rich industrialist, wielded tremendous influence, whilst Milner was sympathetic to the strained circumstances of the Uitlanders.

President Steyn of the Orange Free State and a large group of aggressively-minded Cape Colony Afrikaners were ready to support President Kruger.

WAR INEVITABLE

<hr/>

K NOWING that he could rely on German support, President Kruger delivered an ultimatum to the British on 9 October 1899. It was rejected by Britain two days later, and the Boers began to invade British territory.

Prior to the outbreak of hostilities, during the period of tension, the Boers were being supplied with large quantities of arms by the Germans, through Delagoa Bay.

This armament consisted of numerous martini and mauser small arms, accurate long-range lightweight guns of devastating destructive power, and other war material.

The Boers were fully confident about taking on the might of the British Army.

The conflict, known as the South African Anglo-Boer War, was conducted over vast tracts of very difficult terrain.

The British Army was led by generals and officers of professional military experience, gained in campaigns in Afghanistan, the Crimea, India and the Sudan.

They were expecting a straightforward military victory. And the fact that they were being opposed by an army of mainly Boer farmers and settlers, who were deemed to be unprofessional and therefore easily subdued opponents, only strengthened the British Army's optimism.

Everyone, from the mainly jingoistic British public at

home and in the Cape, to the combatant senior officers and Government, felt that the conflict would soon end, and all of the forces would return to Britain as conquering heroes.

But the war dragged on, mainly due to the commando tactics of the Boers, a force of highly-trained and dedicated men with particular skills in horse-riding, ambushing and marksmanship.

The British infantry, on the other hand, although very brave and skilled, were restrained by their traditional training in military conflict.

The accent was on solid line formation, rigid dependence on commands, firing in volleys on command only, and bayonet skirmishes in mainly concentrated formations.

An added imposition was the British Army's preference for often long strenuous marches in full kit, in hostile terrain, in extreme temperatures, sometimes culminating in a military action.

Conversely, the Boer marksmen usually kept their ponies well hidden at any scene of ambush.

At the slightest sign of any serious trouble, they could very quickly mount up and ride off into well-covered thorn and scrub areas where it was extremely difficult to attempt any pursuit.

Casualties soon rose to an unacceptable level. For example, War Office figures published on 12 December 1900 revealed more than 11,000 dead (with no list of wounded), including 7,000 dying from dysentery, enteric and other diseases.

As far as the British were concerned, the war was not

proceeding as planned. The reputations of senior Army officers were also being affected.

This culminated in the criticism of the Commander of the Army Corps, General Sir Redvers Buller, by the British High Commissioner, Lord Milner.

He sent a scathing despatch referring to Buller's handling of his campaign to the British Cabinet.

It resulted in Lord Frederick Roberts,VC, taking over command of the British South African Forces.

A distinguished soldier, a veteran of the Afghanistan and India conflicts, he had been promoted to Field Marshal, and Commander-in Chief in Ireland.

He had been to the Cape previously in 1881 and, as trouble had arisen at that time, he was appointed to command the British Forces.

Gladstone's Government, however, came to terms with the Boers and Roberts was ordered home after only 24 hours in Cape Town.

The Boers continued their military successes, and disastrous campaigns befell the British Army one after another, in regular fashion.

Lord Roberts' son, Lieutenant Frederick Roberts, was mortally wounded at the battle of Colenso while attempting to limber up one of the British field guns that had been temporarily abandoned at the height of the battle.

During the action, a party of volunteer stretcher bearers included the young Mahatma Gandhi, then a struggling young legal advocate. He was also a member of the Natal Indian Congress Party.

Lord Roberts' attitude to the Boers was widely held to have been influenced by the death of his son.

Nora, his wife, who had accompanied him to South Africa, was said to have been gravely upset, and she had a formidably sharp tongue and an intimidating personality.

Her grief for her son manifested itself in her hostility, unforgiving vengefulness and uncompromising attitude to all Afrikaners.

On his appointment to Supreme Command, and eventually with the assistance of numerous colonial forces, Roberts proceeded to roll up the Boer resistance.

In February 1900, the long siege at Ladysmith, enforced by Boers, was lifted.

Back in the UK, the public were ecstatic with delight.

In London, newspaper vendors were vigorously shouting the news "Ladysmith relieved".

General Buller, despite previous criticism, had been permitted to stay as Field Commander in Natal, and was responsible for the relief at Ladysmith. He received the following telegram from Queen Victoria: "Thank God for news you have telegraphed to me. Congratulate you and all under you with all my heart. V R I."

The young Winston Churchill was also present at the lifting of the Ladysmith siege.

Well-known for his news bulletins transmitted to the newspapers at home, sometimes with a blunt but always truthful comment, Churchill dispatched a radical communication to the Morning Post.

He expressed his admiration for the Boer fighting man's

qualities, quantifying his fighting skills as being worth those of three to five regular soldiers.

This caused considerable offence to the jingoistic British public.

In further fostering general disapproval, and in an appeal for magnanimity, he added a wish that a generous and forgiving policy be followed toward the Boers.

Although this went against the grain of national feeling, Churchill was generally forgiven for his enlightened views because of his heroic, patriotic, pro-Empire status.

Field Marshal Roberts achieved success by the use of new strategies, and the arrival of very large forces of British and colonial contingents, and some naval brigades.

A series of temporary armed forts and camps, at reasonably short intervals, and telegraph communications, were set up. Railways were used, and many trained cavalry units were employed to help counter the Boer tactics.

The most infamous measures were the burning and blowing-up of many Boer farms, plus the confiscation of cattle and crops.

The British also intimidated some of the Boers into signing or swearing oaths of future non-violence towards the British.

But the most reprehensible strategy was the construction and planning of concentration camps.

They were used to incarcerate mainly women and children, and their black workers – mostly victims and refugees of the farm burnings.

The punitive measures continued when Lord Kitchener

became Commander-in-Chief in November 1900. Lord Roberts, on relinquishing command, returned to England where Victoria made him a Knight of the Garter, a prestigious and rare honour. And she gave him an earldom.

Parliament voted him an award of £100,000 and, on being invited to dine with the Queen at Buckingham Palace, he was escorted en route and more than 14,000 troops lined the streets.

Hundreds of thousands of citizens cheered and clapped him, shouting "Bravo Bobs", the name by which he was popularly known.

Meanwhile, in South Africa, the situation in the camps and the privations of the so-called Boer refugees had remained comparatively secret.

Eventually, news began to filter through, especially in the Cape Town area, of the deaths of many women and children in the camps.

The camps were partly used for refugees, but functioned mainly as internment camps.

They were referred to as "concentration camps" because of the necessity to concentrate Boer families, including women, children and black workers, some of whom had been associated with men who were away, possibly on commando raids.

The camps bore no comparison with the later Nazi concentration camps and the systematic torture, forced slave labour, starvation and death by neglect, disease, shooting and gassing.

But, by a tragic coincidence, though under different circumstances, death and disease in the Boer Camps had a loose connection with the latter.

On 23 March 1901, the world began to learn of the starvation of the Boers in British concentration camps.

In April, Mr St John Broderick, then Secretary for War, in response to worldwide criticism, told the House of Commons that Sir Alfred Milner was giving his personal attention to an attempt to improve conditions in the camps.

This attempt at reassurance was greeted with great scepticism, certainly by many opposition members (mainly Liberals) in the House, as well as by a few members of the general public outside.

Having been aware earlier, (in the late 1900s) of the privations of the Boer women and children, Emily Hobhouse embarked on the idea, and organisation of, a relief fund.

The war was then thought to have been practically over, but it was to blow up again, and last much longer.

Emily named the fund The South African War Distress Fund For Women And Children.

To launch the fund and place it on a solid footing, Emily enlisted the help and advice of Leonard Courtney MP.

After demanding to know "What could we hope to collect?" and "Would the military allow relief?" he finally gave his blessing to the launch.

The fund was described thus: "Character: Benevolence, Non Party, Political or Denominational. Aim: To feed, clothe, shelter, rescue and help, without wounding self-respect. Scope: Women and children in all areas affected by the War, irrespective of Nationality or race. Distribution: The aim, not only to succour, but also to soften embittered feelings, the distribution should be placed in the hands of persons deputed by the Committee to be given, after due consideration."

The British Government, in agreeing to the launching of the fund, expressed reservations lest supplies should filter through to Boers who were fighting the British.

Nevertheless, the Government's consent was a great encouragement to the aims of the Fund Committee and titled and other society people were invited to help.

Emily's remarks about these efforts are quite revealing: "It was quite an education interviewing influential people, and I am afraid to say, it modified adversely my too idealistic view of human nature."

The committee's composition was as follows: Chairman, Sir Thomas Acland; Treasurer, Lady Farrer; Secretary, C E Maurice.

With a working committee, and interested supporters including Sir Edward Fry, Herbert Spencer, the Bishop of Nottingham, and the Marchioness of Ripon, Lady Rendel, the fund got off to a positive start.

THE POLITICAL SCENE

———◆———

O N 17 October 1900, the Tories, under Lord Salisbury, had been re-elected with a landslide majority of 401 seats against an opposition of 268. Election fever added fuel to a general feeling of pride in the Empire, and further expansionism.

The Boer War was the pervading issue during the run-up to the election.

The Government severely criticised the Opposition, claiming that they lacked patriotism. In response, the Opposition generally accused the Government of exploiting war fever.

Throughout the country, the atmosphere was electric.

Bands of youths, carrying banners with slogans, thronged the cities and towns of suburbia, loudly singing jingles such as: "Vote, boys, vote for Harry Hopkins / He's the man whose going to win / We'll vote for all we can / For old Harry is our man / And we'll try our best to get him in."

Many women, too, were caught up in the national fervour. Although it was considered unladylike to patrol the streets, many women supported the committees for and against the conduct of the war.

On October 29, The City Of London Imperial Volunteers returned from the Boer campaign and were greeted by a vast crowd of jubilant citizens. The soldiers were welcomed by the Lord Mayor of London at the Guildhall.

Charitable funds supported by events such as fetes and bazaars were set up by many society ladies.

The proceeds were used to help wounded and disabled soldiers who had participated in the conflict, which appeared to be drawing to its conclusion.

As well as launching her own fund, Emily had become involved in politics.

The expected peace did not come to fruition, as guerrilla warfare was extremely difficult for the British soldiers to contain.

Having too many infantrymen in tight formation, with associated heavy equipment, proved to be a hazard and resulted in many casualties.

President Steyn was still active in the field with his much experienced General de Wet.

President Kruger, who had left the Transvaal shortly after its annexation by the British, was in Europe.

However his general officers – Botha, de la Rey, Smuts, and Viljoen – continued to be an active and very serious threat to British military supremacy.

There had already been a serious proposition, mainly by some members of the Liberal Opposition and supported by members of the Irish Home Rule group, for conciliation with the Boers.

Emily's uncle, Henry Hobhouse MP, wrote to the Daily Chronicle on 15 September 1899, referring to the abortive enquiry into the Jameson Raid: "It is impossible not to feel that the Boers of the Transvaal have reason to be very suspicious of all the proposals, coming from our side, to alter the status of affairs, and to hesitate long before accepting them. To suppose that they can resist by arms is preposterous, nothing but useless bloodshed, and fresh excesses of exasperated feeling could come of such resistance."

Leonard Courtney, the Liberal MP for South East Cornwall (although he was to be displaced in the General Election), supported conciliation with the Boers.

He had been asked to speak on the subject at various venues, but first he decided to address his own constituents.

The day after hostilities began, on 12 October 1899, at a meeting in Liskeard, near St Ive, Cornwall, he expounded his views regarding conciliation.

The local Cornishmen, despite giving him a passive hearing, decided they could not support his resolution of "regret of war".

The public rebuff spelt out a dim political future for him. By November 1899, Courtney and some of his associates, in view of some varying Liberal opposition to hostilities against the Boers, launched a South African Conciliation Committee. Courtney was elected president.

He had been a longstanding friend of the Hobhouse family, who lived in his constituency.

An ex Cambridge Don, he had trained as a barrister, worked for The Times newspaper, and had held various Governmental positions.

Courtney had also been considered for the office of Speaker of the House of Commons.

He settled instead for being out of office, taking part in any matters that concerned him.

He believed in proportional representation, and was a zealous worker in supporting women's rights.

He also studied the South African and the Transvaal situations very closely.

The aims of the South African Conciliation Committee were to compromise and to maintain, in the eyes of the general public, the necessity for persons of Dutch and British extraction to live together in relative harmony.

Emily joined the conciliation movement and gave it her wholehearted support.

Meanwhile, Lord Roberts was beset with problems. As he continued to disperse armed Boer formations, he did not realise they intended to prolong their struggle by organising spasmodic guerrilla resistance – a method of warfare that has proven effective against many an invader.

Roberts was perplexed that despite apparent surrenders, and despite promises of non-resistance, some Boers were soon re-engaging in activities such as destroying railway lines, embankments, and viaducts, thus cutting supply and communication facilities.

On March 15 1900, a proclamation was made that burghers must lay down their arms and take an oath of non-belligerence.

Another proclamation, on June 1, declared that, inasmuch that the Orange River Colony was now British territory, all inhabitants thereof, "found in arms, within fourteen days, would be liable to be dealt with as rebels, and to suffer in person and property accordingly".

This proclamation of annexation caused great resentment among the Boers.

It meant that in the event of any sabotage of the railway system, local inhabitants would be held responsible for aiding and abetting, even if they were not involved in any way.

Threats were made that hostages would be forced to ride on the trains, and houses would be burned in the vicinity of such incidents.

Those who were to suffer from the latter were not the mobile commandos, but people who had already surrendered, and were pursuing a peaceful existence.

In August, after it was found that some of the surrendered burghers were resuming hostilities, a new proclamation was declared to the Transvaalers.

It stated that personal safety, and freedom from molestation, were no longer guaranteed, except to burghers who had taken the oath, and that, with the same exception, passes would no longer be issued to enable burghers to return to their homes.

All burghers who had not taken the oath would be regarded as prisoners of war, and transported, or otherwise dealt with. Lord Roberts proceeded to declare that "buildings harbouring the enemy would be liable to be razed to the ground". He added that "burghers failing to acquaint the British with the presence of the enemy, upon their farms, would be regarded as aiding and abetting".

These draconian measures, and growing commando resistance, progressively increased the refugee and prisoner-of-war numbers.

Conditions in the camps, due to the tremendous explosion in refugee and detainee numbers, became a major problem in South Africa.

Figures quoted in The Times History Of The War were as follows: "May 1901 – 77,000 white, 21,000 coloured people in concentration camps. October 1901 – 118,000 and 43,000 respectively detained."

The burghers were able to make a political issue of this, and of the sufferings of their women and children, both in the UK and Europe.

The known camps, in alphabetical order, included: Aliwal North, Balmoral, Barberton, Belfast, Bethulie, Bloemfontein, Brandfort, Edenburg, Harrismith, Heidelburg, Heilbron, Howick, Irene, Johannesburg, Kimberley, Klerksdorp, Krommelleborg, Kroonstad, Krugersdorp, Ladybrand, Ladysmith, Mafeking, Merebank, Middleburg, Mooi River, Nauwpont, Norval's Pont, Pietermaritzburg, Pietersburg, Port Elizabeth, Potchefstroom, Springfontein, Standerton, Vereeniging, Vredefort Road, Vryburg and Wybergh.

There were also prison camps, mainly for Boer combatants, in Bermuda, Ceylon, India, and St Helena.

Such was the massive government and military administrative responsibility undertaken during the course of the hostilities.

The vast resources needed included catering and provisions, maintenance personnel, trains and shipping, guards, doctors, nurses and general administrators. It was a formidable and expensive undertaking.

Portugal, as a long-standing British ally, helped with the incarceration of some of the Boer prisoners in its own camps.

The influence of King Carlos and his more responsible politicians maintained an attitude of consistent friendliness, worthy of their long standing alliance with the British nation.

The imposition of martial law came about very early in the South African campaign.

When the Boer forces invaded British territory, they found it was not altogether a hostile theatre of operations.

Both in Natal and the Cape Colony, the Boer forces met up with many active, and secret, sympathisers.

The majority of the people of Boer extraction joined in the crusade of the Boer invaders.

As well as being invaded, the Mandated Authorities had a rebellion to contend with.

This situation demanded that Martial Law should be declared, especially for the protection of the pro-British, and others of various ethnic origins.

The Military Commander has absolute power with the proviso that he should use his powers in good faith, to ensure the safety of the general public, and the troops serving under him. But as the Military Commander remains answerable to his own Government, he can find himself in an unenviable position.

Such befell both Lord Roberts and his successor, General Kitchener, in their attempts to alleviate the situation.

Their intention might have been only to clear the way for pursuit and defeat of the enemy, but they created a major refugee problem which resulted in death and disease.

A clampdown on news of despondency would also have been necessary. Thus a military system of censorship was enforced.

This, of course, could not prevent news of casualties in both the armed forces and the refugee population becoming public.

Farm Burning

I N HER book The Brunt Of The War And Where It Fell, Emily Hobhouse quoted certain articles of the Hague Convention, first convened at the Hague in the Netherlands in 1899, just prior to the outbreak of the Anglo Boer War. The articles were:

XLIV – Any compulsion of the population of occupied territory to take part in military operations against its own country is prohibited.

XLV – Any pressure on the population of occupied territory to take the oath to the hostile power is prohibited.

XLVI – Family honour and rights, individual lives and property, as well as religious convictions and liberty, must be respected. Private property cannot be confiscated.

XLVII – Pillage is formally prohibited.

L – No general penalty, pecuniary or otherwise, can be inflicted on the population, on account of the acts of individuals for which it cannot be regarded as collectively responsible.

These articles are so specific that any deviation from them would be construed as an act of flagrant disregard. But the articles were not respected in various incidents of the war.

The Boers split into groups of commandos of various

numbers and strengths. They formed an elusive force that was extremely difficult to deal with. Sabotage of rail, telegraph, bridge and road communications systems, by an elusive enemy, were a constant source of disruption to British army units.

Many apparently non-belligerent burghers and farmers were disposed to putting aside their agricultural implements, picking up a hidden Martini rifle, and sniping at British soldiers, especially officers.

There were also quite a large number of foreign nationals, including Dutch or Germans, who were bringing a state of anarchy to some of the larger towns.

One such group, headed by a German, Hans Cordau, who had previously taken the oath of allegiance, was found to have been plotting to burn down houses in Pretoria.

Under cover of the ensuing disruption, senior army officers were targeted to be assassinated, and the Commander - in-Chief, Lord Roberts, was designated to be kidnapped and held hostage.

The group of anarchists were arrested on discovery of the plot. Cordau, having been found to have conclusive documentary evidence as to his involvement in the plan, was tried and summarily shot after being blindfolded and led to a wooden chair.

After his death, he had left behind a personal letter, fully admitting the proposed acts of terrorism.

Another example of the state of anarchy at the time, "The Racecourse Plot" became known to the Military Commissioner of Police in Johannesburg on July 13 1900.

On the following day a large number of foreign nationals, sympathetic to the Boers, had plotted to seize the town.

The small British garrison would have been depleted on that particular day.

Many officers and other ranks were known to be attending an out-of-town race meeting.

The foreigners, who also included a number of disloyal British nationals previously having been on Boer commando raids, were plotting with Boer elements in the town.

Becoming aware of the gravity of the situation, the Military Governor deputised Major F J Davies to arrest all those known to be implicated.

The measures adopted proved to be effective. 364 British and neutral subjects were made prisoners of war, 475 disaffected foreigners were deported, and 1,100 foreign subjects were given free passage to their homelands, by way of recommendation of their respective consuls.

Emily's references to the Hague Convention articles, and the military's lack of respect for them, have formed an excuse, quoted in The Times History Of The War In South Africa, Volume 6: "The Hague Conference of 1899 had codified certain laws, but time had not permitted these rules to be embodied in military regulations."

This supposed vindication also influenced Lord Roberts' decision to despatch approximately 1,000 Boer women, plus their children, back to the Boer lines, unprotected and with little food or means of support.

This brought incalculable chaos to the whole South African campaign.

Also quoted in Emily's publication is a copy of an official military notice:

> The town of Ventersburg has been cleared of supplies and partly burnt, and the farms in the vicinity destroyed, on account of the frequent attacks on the railway line in the neighbourhood. The Boer women and children who are left behind should apply to the Boer commandants for food, who will supply them unless they wish to see them starve. No supplies will be sent from the railway to the town.
> — BRUCE HAMILTON, MAJOR-GENERAL
> NOV 1 1900

Emily adds that very little was heard in England of the farm burning, until May of that year, when accounts by war correspondents and private soldiers began to be published in the British newspapers.

Some of her quotations were quite explicit. For example, The Times correspondent from Bloemfontein reported on April 27 1900 on the activities of a column under the command of Lieut General Sir Reginald Pole-Carew.

The article stated that his column, with definite instructions from Lord Roberts, proceeded to render untenable the farms of such persons who, having surrendered, were still actively supporting the enemy.

Another report by another correspondent, E W Smith in the Morning Leader of April 29 1900, reported two

General Officers, namely French and Pole-Carew at the head of the 18th Brigade and the Guards, marching in and burning almost everything in their advance.

The column was reported as being followed by some 3500 head of loot, namely cattle and sheep, with a mass of hundreds of tons of corn and forage having been destroyed.

Many other reports of farm destruction were reported by Emily, who added that it had become a settled policy of Lord Roberts and that he had earned a similar reputation in Afghanistan where he had previously campaigned and had destroyed a rebel village.

In an appendix to her book, Emily referred to a list of farms burnt during September and October 1901. A total of 105 farms and houses were in the vicinity of the Irene Concentration Camp, giving further evidence of how long this period of destruction lasted.

The Times book stated that Lord Methuen, Commander of the 1st Infantry Division, had destroyed by burning the Boer Commandant de Wet's farm in Roodeport in response to an order from General Roberts.

The book adds: "The policy fitfully adopted after the beginning of June of burning down farmhouses and destroying crops as a measure of intimidation had nothing to recommend it. No other measure aroused such deep and lasting feelings of resentment. Farm burning as a policy of intimidation had totally failed."

The essential object of this war, the imposition of the will of Great Britain upon the Boers by the breaking of their spirit of resistance, was not attained. Complete victory was never an option over the Burghers and their women and children.

Emily Hobhouse, never a person to be complacent, was aware of this in her humanitarian campaign for just treatment of the victims of conflict.

She was a far-sighted woman, light years ahead of her time, whose whole life was devoted to doing good despite much criticism and editorial abuse.

FIELD-MARSHALL RT.HON. EARL ROBERTS OF PRETORIA
V.C., K.G., KP., G.C.B., O.M., G.C.S.I., G.C.I.E.

As Commander-in-Chief, Roberts instituted a Scorched Earth Policy, through farm burning, destruction of chattels, cattle and crops by the British and Colonial Armed Forces.

SHOUTED DOWN

THE NEWS in December 1900 that more than 7,000 men had died of dysentery, enteric fever, and other diseases, with total deaths exceeding 11,000, was in response to a Government debate in July 1900 sparked off by the Conservative MP for Westminster, William Coutts.

He had been asked by The Times to report on medical and hospital arrangements in the colony of the Orange River.

He denounced conditions at the Bloemfontein hospital and spoke of typhoid patients devoid of beds or even stretchers to lie on.

Nursing facilities only consisted of a few untrained and ill-equipped soldiers acting as orderlies, and only three doctors for 400 patients lying in bell tents, with clusters of flies around the whole area.

Coutts alleged that the Government had failed to provide adequate means for safeguarding the general health of the troops.

At last an opportunity arose for the situation to be made public.

His report, when debated in the House of Commons, created uproar, especially in the ranks of the Liberal Opposition.

Amongst the most vehement critics was David Lloyd George, MP for Carnarvon.

Shortly after a particularly heated debate, Lloyd George and Emily travelled to Liskeard, Cornwall, to publicly address the electorate.

To convey the strength of public feeling, the following full report of that meeting is reproduced from The Cornish Times of Saturday 7 July 1900.

Headlined "Peace meeting at Liskeard… Uproarious proceedings… Speakers refused a hearing… Platform stormed… Meeting broken up in disorder", the report read as follows:

A public meeting was held at The Public Hall, Liskeard, on Thursday evening under the auspices of The South African Conciliation Committee in order to advocate an early close of the conflict with the Boers and a settlement which should conciliate the Dutch in the two Republics.

Mr A T Quiller Couch, of Fowey, the well-known novelist, presided, and the speakers were announced to be Miss Ellen Robinson of Liverpool, Miss Emily Hobhouse, Secretary of the Conciliation Committee, and Mr D Lloyd George, The Radical Member for Carnarvon.

The announcement of the meeting caused great interest in the town and district, where political feeling has of late been unusually exalted, and it was anticipated from the first that the proceedings would not pass off without some demonstration of opposition to the views set forth by the Committee.

These expectations proved only too well justified.

From the very beginning the temper of the large audience that filled the Hall was evidently unfavourable to the object of the meeting.

The Chairman had to bring his opening remarks to a hurried conclusion, and after this the crowd practically captured the meeting.

Neither of the lady speakers could gain a hearing for more than a few minutes; Mr Lloyd George was unable even to utter a word, and after a scene of uproar and disorder unparalleled at Liskeard, the platform was stormed by a party of young fellows, many of whom bore miniature Union Jacks, and the meeting was broken up in confusion.

Prior to the meeting "Imperialist" literature was freely distributed to those assembling in the streets around the Hall, and the expectation of a lively gathering attracted a crowded audience within the building.

A good number of ladies were present with numerous residents from country districts, but quite half the Hall was filled with townsmen who, even before the proceedings began, manifested their sentiments by singing and whistling patriotic airs and vociferously cheering Private Webber, of the 2nd DCLI, who came in from Hessenford to attend the meeting wearing his khaki uniform.

The waving of a Union Jack was the signal for renewed cheering, and calls for cheers for Lord Roberts and Buller were readily responded to.

The entrance of the Chairman and speakers was the signal for an outburst of shouting. God Save The Queen was started, and the whole audience, with the occupants of the platform, rose and joined in the singing of the National Anthem.

Vociferous cheers followed for her Majesty, amid the waving of the flag, and after this demonstration the audience settled down for a few minutes, and allowed the Chairman to open the meeting.

Besides Mr Couch and the speakers, those occupying seats on the platform included Mrs Quiller Couch, Mrs J Eliott (Tokenbury), Mr/Mrs Arnold Eliott, Mr and Mrs T Tamblyn, Miss Thompson (Malvern), Miss Impey (Birmingham), Miss Allen, Miss Tregelles, the Misses Williams, Mr J Moon, Mr R Oliver (Polbathic), Rev T Nicholas (St Cleer) and other ladies and gentlemen.

The Chairman, who throughout his speech had to contend with repeated interruption, spoke with great difficulty, and often what he said must have been inaudible except to those in the first few seats.

He said in an ordinary way, he supposed his duty as Chairman would be merely to introduce the speakers, to whom they would listen with more profit than to him, and then sit down and efface himself.

They would agree with him however, that the circumstances were not quite ordinary, and he hoped they would allow him to spend a few minutes in dwelling on the war – (Three cheers for Tommy Atkins and disorder).

The war in South Africa had brought several electors – many electors into sharp opposition to Mr Courtney – (Loud groans and hisses).

58

Mr Courtney had served them long, and was one of whom they had trusted long – ("No more," and uproar).

In the past they had been proud of him and he had reflected back honour on the constituency.

They might tell him that all this was to come to an end, and even if it did so, he thought they could hardly help feeling sorry, for, sad the parting of the ways must be between old friends – (Uproar).

But Mr Courtney did not hide from himself that the war in South Africa, and the diplomacy which prefaced it, had magnified differences which in 1895 might have seemed unimportant to them.

A great wave of what was called Imperialism had swept the country.

It had swept men off their feet or off their heads, he was not quite certain which – ("No, no," and interruption) – and the Liberal Unionist Association of South East Cornwall had turned their back on Mr Courtney – ("Quite right," and loud applause) – and had chosen another candidate for the next general election – (Applause).

They were exercising their undoubted rights; but we too (added Mr Couch) are within our rights to see something heroic in this man – (Derisive laughter).

Mr Courtney was undaunted, undismayed, although his friends fell slowly apart from him and perhaps made him feel more lonely than in truth he was – (Applause and disorder). They (the speakers) were, perhaps, within their rights if they dared to rally round him and bring some encouragement.

He did not know what the speakers who followed him would have to say, but he himself was not a member of the South African Conciliation Committee.

He was merely a private citizen whose judgement refused to approve the war – (Hisses).

But the speakers who were to follow him came to them with higher credentials.

Despising popularity and forgetting party, they had come to speak the truth as they saw it.

The Chairman appealed to the traditions of the borough, to that open-mindedness and sense of respect for the opinions of others which had been the peculiar historical pride of Liskeard in the past, and which, together with their representative, they had the honour of handing over to South East Cornwall in 1885 – (Disorder and voice: "Not in 1900").

Appealing to those traditions, he also put before them the fact that the war they were engaged in was costing them over 100 men and about £750,000 per day.

Those shattered bodies would have to be mourned – (Interruption and a voice: "Spit it out") – the wounded would have to be maintained when they returned.

This great debt would have to be met by them, and if it should occur to them at last that those who so enthusiastically led them into the war had misled them, if it should be borne in upon them that the speakers that evening were right and their popular advisers were wrong, he asked them what would they say to them, supposing they had not spoken against that which they believed to be wrong.

He knew very well what he himself should think.

They were told and a great number in that room seemed to agree, that the time was not convenient for speech; but their political opinions, whether they were right or wrong, could only command respect as they had the courage to enunciate them – ("Hear, hear") – They had been going through a very dark time; they had been derided, menaced, heaped with vulgar abuse, and denied the name of patriots.

This had been a very dark hour, and how many impregnable positions had been lost simply for the lack of a voice to call to them through the darkness' – (Interruption and blowing of a tin trumpet).

At this point someone started Soldiers Of The Queen, and the song was continued to an accompaniment of stamping feet, whistling, cat calls and other noises.

One prominent gentleman mounted a chair and waved a red, white and blue flag, and at times "conducted" the singing, using the banner as a baton.

Cheers were loudly given for some of our Generals in South Africa, with hoots for Kruger and further cheers of "Joe Chamberlain".

Sheer fatigue alone put a stop to the "music" for a time.

Taking advantage of the lull, the Chairman continued his speech.

"Let me assure you," he said, but was interrupted by someone shouting "Give somebody else a chance".

"When the day comes," Mr Couch continued, "and it shows the Liberal position still held, there will be plenty of you to do the shouting, but it will be the men who stand together now who will be able to look each other in the face."

Here the whistling and stamping broke out anew, and the squeaking of the tin trumpet added another discordant element.

Mr Quiller Couch remained standing for a minute or so, and then asked Miss Robinson to address the audience, and hoped they would treat her with the respect a lady deserved.

Miss Robinson arose, and for a few moments comparative quiet prevailed.

She said: "It is very evident that many of us in this room are of different opinions about many things, but I expect there is one thing we are heartily agreed on and that is a love for our native land – (Loud applause).

"I do not suppose there is a single one of the boys at the back of the room, who are making such a noise, who does not love his native country, but perhaps they have a different idea of what their native country ought to be.

"In my younger days we loved England because we felt she held the first place amongst the nations.

"We believed her to be the champion of justice, liberty and humanity, because we thought Englishmen were always fair and just, and that our country was the refuge of the weak and oppressed.

"We loved her too, because we thought England upheld the standard of religion, to do justice and love mercy, and, -

(Here someone walked up the Hall, and his raising of a flag was the signal for another outburst of shouting which continued for some minutes). Proceeding, Miss Robinson said, although England was sometimes at fault, still we believed she was pursuing that high ideal, and that there was still many in her midst who thought this was the England they loved".

"We are sorry to see a different ideal springing up in the land – a different England springing up, which seems only to worship strength and bigness" – (Interruption).

"We see a country which has, during the last decade, added four million square miles to her territory" – (Loud and continued applause).

"Many of you seem to think that is the true ideal of greatness" – (A long interruption took place here, whilst the chorus of The Absentminded Beggar was repeated several times). Miss Robinson went on: "Some think that is the only ideal of true greatness, and we, alas, hear some of our leading statesmen and some ministers of the Gospel, many of our poets and writers, a great part of the press and nearly all the 'men in the street' as they are called, boast of that ideal of England that she should be big and strong, but that she should be good and just and noble they have no comprehension" – (Disorder).

"There are a great many of our countrymen" – Miss Robinson was interrupted by someone at the back of the Hall starting the National Anthem, followed by other patriotic airs.

For some time there was a perfect hubbub.

Cheers were given for the Queen, our Generals at the front, and Sir Lewis Molesworth.

Someone called for three cheers for Kruger, and loud groans were the result.

During a moment's calm Miss Robinson was indignantly heard to remark: "I have spoken at some hundreds of meetings during the past winter but this is the first one at which" – (The noise that followed almost baffles description).

On two or three occasions she attempted to speak, but each attempt led to a renewal of the disturbance.

Presently someone started the Doxology and it was sung with even more fervour than is often the case in chapel.

When the verse had ended, the undaunted speaker uttered a few words but the humming of the Cornish ballad Trelawny was the next item on the programme.

This was apparently encored, for the air was repeated to the accompaniment of stamping feet.

Many of the audience rose to their feet to watch the noisy proceedings at the back.

The vocal effects continued, punctuated with cheering, a white-haired old "Imperialist" encouraging the "boys" at the back by waving his hat, while the gentleman with the flag beat time.

For ten minutes or so Miss Robinson stood regarding the unruly audience with indignation and contempt. It being manifestly impossible to gain a hearing, she at last resumed her seat.

It was some time before the noise in any way abated; flags were waved, chairs and sticks knocked about, and as a Khaki-clad soldier from the Front tried to leave the building, he was lifted shoulder-high, and this lead to an out-burst: of cheering for "Tommy Atkins".

The Chairman rose to await a lull in the uproar.

Mr J A Baron, who had been so energetic with the flag, mounted on a seat and apparently appealed to the back benches by gesture to hear the Chairman, but his appearance was merely the signal for continued cheering.

Another gentleman who has expressed views in favour of Mr Courtney mounted a chair and attempted to speak, but he found it impossible.

A red, white, and blue flag was pinned on his back, and he was pulled to his seat amid derisive laughter.

The Chairman raised his hand to command order, but the temper of the people was up and nothing could quell the disturbance, and Mr Couch sat down.

When the uproar showed signs of ceasing, Mr Baron mounted a chair and waved a flag on which was a portrait of the Queen.

This was greeted with deafening cheers, after which the noise ceased somewhat, but not enough to allow anyone to speak.

Mr T Dyer crossed the room to expostulate with some of those who were disturbing the meeting, but his interference was strongly resented.

Mr Baron coolly showed him his flag, and uttered some remarks which were inaudible at the top of the room, but which led to another outburst of cheering.

Mr Dyer beat a hasty retreat, but was followed for some distance across the hall by Mr Baron.

Some younger men seemed to be menacing the standard-bearer, and at one time it looked as if a free fight would break out.

The whole audience were on their feet, and some timid ladies in the vicinity at once took flight into the anterooms.

After some time an interval of quiet was restored.

Mr Baron mounted a chair, and he was understood to have asked for a fair hearing for the ladies, but the crowd had taken possession of the meeting and refused to listen to him, and continued to sing the National Anthem and other airs.

He then came to the platform and appealed to the audience to give Miss Hobhouse a hearing, she having been standing a mute spectator of the scene for some minutes.

The disorder having decreased somewhat, Miss Hobhouse said: "I think you will all agree with me that if her Gracious Majesty the Queen to whom you have sung, were present here now, she would be heartily ashamed of her Cornish subjects" – (Uproar).

"I have a great deal that I am anxious to say to you" – (Hisses and groans).

"Will you sit down for a few minutes and listen to me? It seems to me a strange thing that Cornishmen will not listen to a Cornish woman."

A deafening noise followed, and Mr Baron again appealed for "a hearing for the lady".

The Chairman also endeavoured to restore order, and after some time Miss Hobhouse continued with: "Is it your wish that I should address"– but was allowed to go no further.

"I have addressed meetings lately," she continued after two or three minutes' interval, "all over England – in Leicester, Leeds, Bradford, Liverpool and Manchester – but it has remained for me to come to Cornwall to see the worst behaviour of all.

"I am quite sure that is not the best of the Cornish people – ("Hear, hear," from the platform).

"It is only a few thoughtless and foolish spirits" – (Derisive laughter and hoots, and a deep voice at the back of the hall shouted: "How do you find 'em in London?" Stamping of feet again commenced, and Trelawny was hoarsely voiced).

Miss Hobhouse, when she was permitted, thanked the audience for having sung to her the old ballad of her family, but she had heard enough of it.

If they wanted to honour the Queen, let them behave as subjects of the British Empire.

Miss Hobhouse struggled bravely through these sentences but at last she was ineffectual at making her voice heard.

Trelawny and Soldiers Of The Queen were again shouted, and when this was done, Miss Hobhouse indignantly exclaimed, making her voice heard above the din: "it seems strange that the people of Liskeard should allow a few thoughtless and ill-mannered boys to spoil a meeting" – (Disorder).

"But this kind of behaviour," she continued under great difficulty, "will do more to advance our cause than the most eloquent speeches we could deliver.

"The account of this meeting will be printed far and wide through England and Cornish people will be held up to shame, because they would not give a fair hearing, especially to a lady, on this most complicated question" – (Uproar).

"One wonders that the people of the town, and an old respected town like Liskeard, should endure a handful of thoughtless boys to upset their meeting.

"It does not seem creditable.

"You should not have come if you did not intend to give us a hearing, but now that you have, will you give us a fair hearing, and when we have finished, you can ask us many questions, and talk as much as you like.

"Remember," (she added in a voice almost inaudible to the Press) that "manners maketh man." – (Derisive laughter).

Generals Baden Powell and Buller were again cheered at this point, as was also Mr Chamberlain.

When quiet was somewhat restored, Miss Hobhouse said: "It is very strange to me, after so many years of absence" – (Disorder) – "to come again into the old familiar town and to see around me so many familiar faces, and be thus treated.

"It is a sad thought that I should be advocating what I am told are unpopular views in the town.

"But it is still a sadder thing for me to hear that Cornish people feel so differently on this subject from what I conceive to be the right and the noblest thing.

"It is a very great satisfaction to me to have the opportunity of putting before you to some extent, the views I believe are correct" – (Uproar) – "but I ask you to give a quiet hearing, and then go home and think over what I have said.

"We have respect for the feelings of our opponents, and we ask for the same." – (Applause from the platform).

"It is impossible, on an evening like this, to touch on more than one or two points on so great and complicated a question as that which faces us in the South African problem.

"I thought I should have spoken last and taken up just the shreds of what the other speakers left unsaid, but it has fallen out that I shall put before you just one aspect of the great question as it appears to me.

"A few weeks ago, there was but one word on the lips of the people of London, and in the hearts of the people of England.

"All those" – (A tremendous noise arose, which made it impossible for the speaker to finish the sentence).

Twice she made an attempt to speak, saying she would address the first few rows of people if they could hear.

Rule Britannia was being sung when she made this remark, and when those in the back of the hall thought she was addressing the few in the front, they put more power into their singing, accompanied by continuous stamping.

The Chairman rose to remonstrate, but this was only provocative of another wild outburst of shouting and cheering.

Mr R H Lee mounted a chair and was understood to ask

the audience to give the ladies a hearing. Mr T Peters also addressed a portion of the meeting from the middle of the hall, and was understood to say that the reproaches of the lady speaker were themselves provoking the audience to disorder.

Mr Baron attempted to quell the disturbance, but all efforts were useless.

The Chairman shouted: "Do the respectable people of Liskeard wish the ladies to be insulted? Do they? Why do they allow the meeting to be dictated to by a lot of boys?"

This appeal was unheeded and unheard by the element, and it was not until four burly policemen took up positions near the main entrance that order was in any way restored.

For about ten minutes, Miss Hobhouse was allowed to continue, without interruption, as she spoke of the heroic defence of Mafeking, and the sufferings endured by the besieged.

Loud cheering for the defenders of Mafeking at last drowned her words, and Miss Hobhouse remarked: "Yes, you may well cheer them, they deserve a cheer."

The noise increased, and as the noisy ones saw that the police made no attempt to check them, they resumed their endeavours to break up the meeting, God Save The Queen being once more sung.

Miss Hobhouse continued, but only the reporters could hear her remarks.

"This I say, that those who desecrate the National Anthem by making it the means of interrupting meetings, are the very last people who would ever follow the noble example, which has been set them by the people of Mafeking, and would be the last to uphold their country in time of peril."

Once more, the uproar swelled, someone starting The Englishman and The Death Of Nelson, but both proved unsuccessful, and popular airs were tried.

Miss Hobhouse readdressed her remarks as to the abuse of the National Anthem, particularly to the Press representatives.

After the storm had spent itself somewhat, Miss Hobhouse said: "I have been speaking at meetings – large meetings, to which this is nothing but a private party – in the North of England, and have there, had perfect attention.

"The rest of England will read the account of what has happened tonight, with disgust.

"I shall take away from Liskeard" – (From the back of the Hall rose the strains of Men Of Harlech, with deafening stamping and shouting, and Miss Hobhouse, seeing that any further attempt at speech would be useless, resumed her seat).

A few expressed a wish to hear Mr Lloyd George, but as that gentleman rose to speak, the riot broke out with increased violence.

In fact, it was afterwards stated by leading Conservatives, that the whole of the opposition to the meeting had been aroused by Mr Lloyd George's observations in the House of Commons last Friday, when he attributed most unworthy motives to members of the Government in connection with the war. The Hon Member, as he came forward, was greeted with hoots, cheers, catcalls, shrill whistles, and booing, followed by Soldiers Of The Queen.

The crowd was evidently getting dangerously excited, and many more ladies left the Hall.

Messrs R N Clemens and Baron led further cheering for Balfour, Chamberlain, Buller and others, while Mr Lloyd George stood smiling at the table, but did not attempt to utter a syllable. It was perfectly evident that the crowd would not hear the Welsh MP at any price.

Then came the culmination of the disorder.

About fifty young men of the town, some bearing miniature Union Jacks, gradually worked their way up the Hall, happily on the side furthest from the Press table.

Shouting, cheering, and whistling, they swept up the stairs and surged upon the platform, where they occupied half the space, and kept up a continuous noise of shouting, singing and cheering.

Still Mr Lloyd George refused to give in, and remained standing by the table.

Seeing this, one of the storming party made a dash with a view to overturning the table, but was collared by Mr Arnold Elliot, the local secretary of the meeting, and the attempt was frustrated.

The youths on the platform were good-humoured though noisy, and no attempt was made to molest the speakers.

But most of the chairs were seized and pulled in a heap across the middle of the platform behind the Chairman, who remained seated. Gradually the platform was invaded from the other end, and people were standing on the Press table and on the chairs, all over the room.

Meanwhile, Miss Hobhouse was greeted by several old St Ive friends among the audience, and, with Mrs J Elliot and Miss Robinson, took the opportunity of distributing "Conciliation" leaflets among the people in front.

Many of these were at once torn up and the pieces tossed contemptuously into the air, while Britons Never Shall Be Slaves was sung by the storming party.

Presently, a further demonstration attracted attention to the floor of the Hall.

The Khaki clad soldier from Hessenford was hoisted on to the shoulders of half a dozen men, who carried him around the Hall to the steps leading to the opposite side of the platform, with the evident intention of taking possession of that portion also.

While the tour of the Hall was being made the opposition cheered and shouted frantically.

On reaching the platform steps, the men carrying the soldier found their way barred by a group of men determined to resist a capture of the platform.

One of the group on the platform, a sergeant of police on leave from Devonport and a brother of the soldier, pulled him off the shoulders of the men, and for a moment, a free fight seemed imminent.

No blow, however, was struck, and the disturbers relinquished the idea of storming that side of the platform, and retired to another part of the Hall.

Meanwhile, those who had possession of the platform continued to sing and shout with undiminished vigour.

The proceedings would have passed off without violence had not Mr Lloyd George and Rev T Nicholas moved to the centre of the platform with a view to taking down the barricade of chairs.

In a moment, they were surrounded and rudely hustled, till they retreated again to the front.

But this encounter had stirred the passions of the crowd, and when some of the pro-Boer sympathisers, on the other side of the platform, attempted to pull away the chairs, an ugly rush was made at them.

On both sides the chairs were pulled away and thrown in all directions and as the two parties got within arm's reach several blows were struck.

At this point, the police made their appearance on the platform, and the conflict, at once, ceased.

The ladies with Mr Quiller Couch, Mr Lloyd George and their supporters, were then persuaded to leave the Hall and platform, and the crowd formed a lane and allowed them to walk to the ante-room without molestation.

Cheers for Lord Roberts and leading statesmen followed them.

The mob remained in undisputed possession of the Hall and platform, and for a quarter of an hour longer continued to amuse itself with shouting, singing, and horseplay.

One of the leaders, attempting a vocal solo, approached near the edge of the platform, waving a Union Jack, and fell over into the arms of the people below.

Hoisted up again, amid roars of laughter, he addressed an imaginary Chairman, and then proceeded with his song.

About half past nine, the uproar came to an end, and after once again singing the National Anthem, the gathering dispersed.

One result of the public debacle in Liskeard was the loss of many longstanding friends of the Hobhouse family through what Emily described as a divergence of principle, a situation which left her deeply wounded and regretful.

But the meeting in no way deterred Emily from her humanitarian efforts for the relief of the suffering Boer woman and children.

In view of the competition with the funds being raised for wounded soldiers at home, and their families, Emily's funding efforts were under restraint.

Her Relief Fund was generously supported by the Christian group, The Society Of Friends.

A Visit To The South African Camps

I N A BIOGRAPHY of General Smuts by his son, Emily is described as "a middle-aged Quaker lady". In the light of the help she received from The Society Of Friends, one is tempted to assume the truth of that description. One can see a similarity between Emily's Christian attitude and their ideals.

Founded in England in the 17th Century by George Fox, the basis of the Quaker faith is that every individual who believes has the power of direct communication with the Almighty, who will guide them in the ways of the truth.

A power called the "inner light" is their guide.

They meet as individuals, and remain silent in each other's company, until someone is motivated by the Holy Spirit to impart their particular message.

They believe that violence should be countermanded by gentleness.

As Friends, they refuse to take part in war, even refusing to resist personal violence.

They were the originators of the abolition of slavery, and worked for prison reform and improved education. Their modern acceptance of the Scriptures is now quite liberal.

Quakers continue to refuse to take part in warfare, but are always ready to help the victims of war, by organising relief, helping refugees in distress, or sending their ambulance units into the heat of battle.

It will be seen that Emily Hobhouse, despite the national fervour for war, stuck tenaciously to her principles.

But can any person with such deep convictions be accommodated, or accepted, by their own nation in the middle of a conflict?

The world, and eventually Britain, began to take note of the casualty rates of the women and children in the concentration camps.

Emily gradually became more upset with the inadequacy of the help given to those unfortunates.

She decided, as the year progressed, to take material relief to South Africa herself.

She became tortured by a vision of helpless women and children who were homeless, desperate and distressed.

Many were starving or racked with illness and disease in insufferable conditions.

As money in the distress fund was amassing, both from home and overseas, further finance was also being given to Emily privately.

Finally, deciding to go to South Africa, Emily sought the blessing of her aunt and uncle.

She eventually arrived at Cape Town, and like most visitors, was captivated by the magnificence of the distant peaks, and the view of Table Mountain.

On the same ship on which she travelled was Joshua Rowntree, an eminent Quaker, who was travelling first-class with his wife and nephew.

Rowntree, being a well-known philanthropist, was en route for Natal.

Emily, although having money of her own, travelled second-class.

But she did have one valuable possession – a letter of introduction to Sir Alfred Milner from her aunt, Lady Hobhouse.

One of the reasons for seeing Milner was to gain his permission for Emily to visit some of the camps to organise relief for the suffering women and children.

Martial Law had inhibited travel up-country, and access was only possible if the necessary passes could be produced.

Emily found Lord Milner charming and, up to a point, quite helpful.

During the interview, Milner agreed that the policy of farm-burning had negative effects, including the truckloads of refugee women and children he had seen in the combat areas, which he agreed was most distressing.

Emily pressed the point that the situation was explosive, in that it was generating thousands of anti-British and mainly female martyrs.

She told him that people at home were becoming increasingly disturbed over the accelerating casualty numbers, both civilian and military.

Milner granted permission for Emily to travel to the refugee camps with an interpreter and he agreed to supply two railway trucks to transport her relief supplies.

But he said that in view of the military situation, the final decision rested with the Military Commander, Lord

Kitchener. In the event, Kitchener's reaction was extremely disappointing. He would not allow a companion interpreter, observing that there were plenty available in the Bloemfontein area, the only place to which she would be allowed access.

And he said she could only take one truck full of relief supplies.

On her arrival in Bloemfontein, Emily was welcomed and stayed with a family called Fichardt.

One of the sons had been educated in England, and was a former Mayor of Bloemfontein.

Being wounded, he was taken prisoner near Paardeburg. He had been one of 1,200 Boers who had escaped from Cronje's Laager after being hemmed in by 40,000 British military.

The family were regarded as influential, having accommodated both Kruger and Milner during the conference in 1899.

Fichardt Junior had been senior to Commandant de Wet and was full of accounts of earlier military engagements. Fichardt himself was on parole.

In a further communication to Emily from Government House in Cape Town, Lord Milner said he had requested General Pretyman, the Military Governor of the Orange River Colony, to give her every assistance within his power.

Milner, being responsible for the administration of martial law on the one hand, and being responsible to the British Government on the other, must have found it difficult to offer much help to Emily.

Upon visiting General Pretyman at Government House, Bloemfontein, Emily recalled previous happy times between her family and the Pretymans in Bournemouth.

Emily remembered visiting the Pretymans with her aunts, Cathy and Eliza, and how very shy she had been of the soldier there, now the General.

She was greeted very warmly by the General and told him she needed his permission to stay with the Fichardts, who were in a military zone.

Mrs Fichardt had lost her husband in the pursuit of the war, and her two daughters, one of whom was disabled, were in Cape Town and not allowed to return home to her.

Her two sons were under surveillance, being of military potential.

When the General pointed out that Mrs Fichardt was a bitter woman, Emily agreed, but also countered that her stay could have beneficial effect.

The General agreed there was some substance in Emily's suggestion, and wrote out the permit.

Emily was also given a permanent pass to visit camps in the immediate area of Bloemfontein.

One of her first visits was to a camp two miles outside Bloemfontein.

It was set on the side of a hill in an area of the Veldt scorched in the heat of the sun.

The camp housed almost 2,000 people. Most were women, more than 900 were children, and there were a few "hands-up men" who had surrendered.

The repetitive rows of bell tents, with no named streets

or numbers, led to an inevitable state of confusion. Each tent housed eight to 12, dependant on size, and drew the intense heat of the sun. At night the tents were not insulated from the cold, and during rain or dust storms, the flaps had to be held down.

With hardly any room to move, many of the inmates found the environment claustrophobic.

The water supply was insufficient, soap for washing was non-existent, no mattresses were available, fuel was only to be obtained by cutting from the semi-green, parched scrub on the side of the hill, there were no adequate toilet facilities, and flies swarmed almost everywhere.

Emily was told stories of wet nights, when the water streamed down through the canvas sides, under the tent flaps, and wet their sleeping blankets as they lay on the ground; and of another occasion when a lethal puff adder entered one of the tents.

Insufficient and unsuitable food made the inmates' misery complete.

As if the treatment of those in the camps wasn't bad enough, Britain continued to heap national honours and awards upon the senior officers who had caused the suffering of the women and children.

Emily related the experience of a Mrs Reintjes, a detainee in the camp, who had six sick children – two in the hospital section with typhoid fever, the other four in her tent.

Not only that, but her husband was a prisoner in Ceylon, she was pregnant, and the birth was imminent.

Mrs Reintjes told Emily she had the means to support herself and her family either in the town, or in the colony where she had relatives.

She would gladly have returned to her farm, which had not been burnt, although all her furniture had been destroyed. But instead of being allowed freedom to fend for herself and her children, she was forced to stay in the camp, while her little ones were fading away.

Emily described her plight as absolute cruelty, of which England should be ashamed.

She said the authorities were at their wits' end, with no idea of how to cope with such grave circumstances.

She blamed crass male ignorance, helplessness, muddling through, and stupidity on the part of the camp administrators.

Emily admitted that she melted towards them a little when, in a humble manner, they confessed that the whole situation was one massive blunder.

Many went on to say that they had been presented with an insoluble problem, and did not really know how to deal with it.

The Major in charge said he was severely curtailed by having no finance, no trucks, insufficient quantities of supplies of every description, and no powers to deal with the situation as he would like to have done.

Being in overall charge of the camps in the once Free State, he added that the demand for clothing in places such as Rhenoster drove him to despair.

He also implored Emily to join him in writing a letter to

General Kitchener, requesting that she be permitted to go further North, where camp conditions, it was said, were horrendous.

Apart from having a serious effect on the morale of the military administrators, the whole camp system had placed thousands in physical jeopardy, in conditions they were unable to endure.

The daily prescribed allowance for each person over six in the camps, were as follows: 8oz meat, 8oz meal, rice or potatoes, half an ounce of coffee, 3oz sugar, 1oz salt, and one-twelfth of a tin of condensed milk.

As even that daily allowance was not always supplied in those quantities, it was considered a starvation diet.

And because cooking oil, or fat, or indeed fresh vegetables were not included, it was also grossly inadequate from a nutritional point of view.

Small retail shops were permitted in some camps, where a limited number of commodities such as soap, not supplied by the army, commanded exorbitant prices.

With negative incomes, rare commodities such as a reel of cotton, priced at sixpence (an enormous sum in those times), were beyond the means of most mothers.

On January 30 1901, Emily had a long interview with General Pretyman.

The General was due to relinquish his command to a Major Goold-Adams.

This downgrading of responsibility, from a General to a Major, suggests that less importance was being given to the area, in view of the military conflict proceeding elsewhere.

General Pretyman, under pressure from Emily over the state of camps under his governorship, asked Emily her opinion of the refugee situation.

She replied that she thought the women should be sent back to their homes – and the sooner the better.

Emily also suggested their release should be gradual, as a mass dispersal could cause further problems.

The General agreed, and was obviously very relieved at being allotted a less controversial command.

But he reminded Emily, that, under the circumstances, he was powerless to act any further.

However, in a private letter to Sir Alfred Milner, on the the following day, 31 January 1901, the General said that Emily was very much in sympathy with "our enemies".

The General said he found her a pleasant, well-educated woman to talk to, but found her misguided in her love for the Boers in general.

Had she been aware of the content of the letter at the time, Emily would have insisted on her "love for the Boers" being altered to "love for suffering human beings".

In a similar vein, Major John Hamilton Goold-Adams, the newly-appointed Lieutenant Governor, wrote to Milner on 9 February 1901 to complain that Miss Hobhouse, together with Mrs Steyn, Miss Fleck and Mrs Fichardt, were causing a great deal of unrest by relating the hardships the inmates were enduring.

He also stated that he had it on good authority (one wonders, in such a military situation, who this could possibly be?) that Emily was there on behalf of the Liberal

Party to collect information for them, for what Goold-Adams called "the usual purposes".

It is a fact that Emily had become quite friendly with the three Boer women, but that did not mean she was sympathetic to the Boers' aggression, or had any political motive.

Maynie Fleck, with whom Emily had become acquainted, was quite a young girl who had previously worked at Bloemfontein prison providing clothing and other necessities for the desperately needy Boer prisoners.

She had been described as rather a saucy and fearless patriot. Isabel Steyn, a refined Boer woman, was the prisoner wife of President Steyn. She was constantly accompanied by an armed British soldier, who always stood outside any house or establishment that she entered, in a custodial mode with a fixed bayonet.

Emily struck up a friendship with this dignified woman. They much later became dear friends, but always addressed each other in their correspondence as Miss Hobhouse or Mrs Steyn and were never on first-name terms.

Emily, prior to her next visit to the camp at Norvals Pont, did refer to the response of the Bloemfontein Camp internees.

She stated that they were under the impression that she possessed some sort of divine influence and could solve their problems and set them free.

But, like the army officers, she only had limited facilities at her disposal.

Meanwhile, a fund launched by the Lord Mayor of London, the Mansion House Fund, was founded to help the Uitlander refugees. Many soldiers were under the impression that the fund was helpful to the Boer refugees as well, which was not the case.

One form of positive help was given by General Pretyman to Emily before he left his Governorship.

He gave Emily authority to arrange the sterilisation and supply of drinking water to the refugees with associated utensils, all paid for by the Treasury.

Additionally, Captain Hume, temporary camp Commandant at Bloemfontein, had been delegated to assist Emily with any reasonable help she required.

She observed that the Captain insisted that all the inmates had come to the camp for protection, and should be grateful for being there.

Emily insisted, on occasions, that the Captain should accompany her in her ministrations to the sick and dying.

On one such visit, when the Captain was with Emily, he saw a dying child, who was just skin and bone. He looked at the pathetic child skeleton and, melting a little, conceded that it was awful to see such a little one in so much suffering.

L S Amery, writing in The Times History Of The War In South Africa, in 1907, offers a balanced review of the adoption of the camps, as follows:

It will be seen that the policy was inspired by two motives.

In the first place, it was supposed that the removal of the families would induce fighting Boers to surrender, and would thus shorten the war.

In the second place, it was a measure of humanity towards the unprotected occupants of lonely farms.

The decision was taken somewhat lightly.

In its primary object, it failed absolutely.

Far from providing an inducement to surrender, it lifted from the fighting burghers a load of embarrassment. To the British, the military consequences were disastrous.

To the Boers, the gain was twofold.

On the shoulders of their enemy lay the heavy tasks of removal and maintenance, involving enormous expense, and a grave hindrance to military operations, while they themselves, relieved of all responsibility for their women and children, were free to devote their energies with a clear conscience to the single aim of fighting.

While one of the British aims was signally defeated, the other, that of humanity, was at first only partially attained. The scheme for the concentration camps was lacking in foresight.

Adequate provision was not made for the hosts of refugees requiring shelter. The regular medical and sanitary staff were already fully occupied with the needs of the army, and men were lacking organisation and supervision of the camps. Sites, on purely military grounds, often proved wholly unsuitable.

Amery proceeds to castigate the Boer inmates of the camps for "being utterly averse to cleanliness and ignorance of the simplest elements of medicine and sanitation. The result was that for a certain period, there was a very high rate of mortality among these unfortunate people". This is where, it can be argued, the statement by Amery loses its impartiality.

In many camps, overcrowding, lack of supplies of disinfectants, soap, clear fresh water, inadequate toilets, removal of refuse and washing facilities, were bound to have a debilitating effect on even the least sanitary-minded occupant.

The incidence of such illnesses as pneumonia, pleurisy and bronchitis, to name but a few, are certainly not the result of lack of hygiene.

Johanna "Hansie" van Warmelo, a volunteer nurse at Irene Concentration Camp, described the conditions imposed upon such Boer inmates in her camp.

She cited the case of a Mrs Pretorius, whose five children were ill with dysentery. She was forced to nurse her children all night long in the dark, without even a candle to afford a glimmer of light.

Her problems were made worse by not having even a scrap of soap to clean their soiled linen.

The claim of Boer indifference to hygiene cannot be substantiated when such horrific conditions were imposed upon them.

Emily's involvement in hygiene conditions within the camps, and her efforts to improve health standards, are too numerous to list, but one example may suffice.

On January 31 1901, in discussion with Captain Hume and Doctor Pern at the Bloemfontein Camp, Emily suggested the use of a large railway boiler to boil the water being drawn from the nearby Modder river, in an effort to eliminate typhoid. She also suggested a wash-house should be installed with adequate water, soap and buckets to alleviate the filthy conditions of the inmates of the camp, with facilities to wash clothing, some of which had remained filthy for months on end.

She was supported by the doctor, and Emily suggested a Superintendent Matron to assist generally.

Nurses and medical supplies had already been requested from the Cape Town authority.

Emily had already decided that the funds of her Relief Society should help nourish, cleanse, or give warmth to the needy inmates.

In all, Emily was only permitted to visit five Camps, including Bloemfontein.

On each visit, she found herself surrounded with hundreds of inmates. Despite language difficulties, she set up or joined various local committees who were eager to help ease the camp conditions.

Despite her own limited resources, many of these people looked upon Emily to bring about the end of their suffering.

Although she could hardly do so, it did nothing but good for them to witness the presence of such a helpful, kind, and understanding woman.

That, in no small way, helped to ease their fears and hatred of the British military occupiers.

Many of the inmates addressed Emily, despite the language difficulty, as "Sister".

In early February, Emily succeeded in visiting two other

camps at Norvals Pont and Aliwal North. Both, according to her, were reasonably well organised and well laid out, with smaller numbers of inmates.

Captain du Plat Taylor, the Camp Commandant at Norvals Pont, had been reprimanded for extravagance.

His misdemeanour was to order £150 of clothing to be distributed to the needy children of the inmates.

The enlightened Captain had also arranged for fresh water to be piped from a spring on a farm nearby.

At Aliwal North, Emily was made welcome by the Camp Commandant, Major Apthorpe. He was quite humanitarian in his administration, with inmates allowed access to the nearby towns of Smithfield, Rouxville and Zastron.

An atmosphere of goodwill appeared to prevail. A local mayor, leading a small committee including a local doctor, had formed a liaison with the camp authority.

Emily distributed much-needed clothing at both camps.

However, the situation at Aliwal North was in stark contrast to the atmosphere at the Bloemfontein Camp when Emily returned.

In mid February, General Pretyman had been succeeded by Major John Hamilton Goold-Adams.

In adopting a more stringent attitude, the army surrounded the local market and ordered the locals to show their passes.

Those who had mislaid their permits were either summarily fined or imprisoned.

At about the same time, the locally-hated Provost

Marshall and his soldiers had surrounded and entered a boarding house belonging to a Mrs du Toit, the wife of a deported Minister of the local church. All the rooms were, without ceremony, forcibly entered and searched in the late-night raid, much to the terror of the occupants.

The soldiers were, so they claimed, looking for the Boer leader de Wet who was reputedly hiding in the area.

Emily herself was not exactly travelling in comfort, accompanied by her railway truck of relief supplies.

The trucks, some roofed and others not, were basically uninsulated and uncomfortable box cars.

Hard springing and the sometimes very tight curves they encountered resulted in severe jolting and a dreadful noise.

The remainder of the trucks were for the troops and their equipment. Sometimes they were forced to stand or crouch for many miles.

The guard's van was usually maintained to a standard regarded as suitable for an NCO, but still offered only a basic, uncomfortable, back-ache-inducing upright position for the weary traveller.

Emily said that on one such occasion, after travelling over very long distances in a continual bolt-upright position, she arrived more dead than alive.

On the way, the ladies' waiting rooms at the remote stations were either locked or converted into temporary offices for the military.

Emily had experienced 15 hours of shunting, jostling, cold, and general discomfort, with only a cold beverage drink for sustenance.

In early March 1901, Emily visited the camp at Springfontein.

She found the camp Commandant, Major Gostling, sympathetic to the needs of the camp internees, but he was severely inhibited through a serious shortage of material supplies.

But Emily was able to supply clothing, to the delight of the inmates, mostly mothers and children.

She also made a successful appeal to some of the local inhabitants, who responded enthusiastically.

A total lack of fuel only compounded the problems of the inmates.

When Emily visited the Kimberley camp, she discovered that the Camp Commandant, Major Wright, was a local colonial volunteer.

He was a rather coarse, lazy and indifferent old man who did not visit the camp for days on end, and had appointed his own son as the camp non-commissioned officer.

The camp covered a very small overcrowded area, with accommodation tents in extremely close proximity to one another.

A repugnantly-smelly and neglected atmosphere pervaded the camp.

Whooping cough was rampant among the children, fuel was in very short supply, and a camp doctor, an Army officer, seemed ignorant of children's ailments.

The despondent community was confined within a very high barbed-wire perimeter fence, with armed sentries at the entrance gate.

To add to the misery of the inmates, there was the very heavy overnight dew, which, condensing on the tent fabric, penetrated the canvas, making the interiors of the tents cold and wet.

During the day, all the blankets and clothing had to be moved to the paths and roadways in an attempt to dry them in the sun.

The authorities had spent £500 on the erection of the easily-penetrable fence but had made no provision for fuel, mattresses or soap for the inmates.

Whilst Emily was visiting the camp, she was upset to see three child corpses being photographed for the benefit of their absent fathers.

One small comfort to Emily was a meeting with a small committee of Kimberley Afrikaners who had helped alleviate the suffering of the women and children.

After the distribution of clothing and other items of aid from her own resources, Emily called on General Pretyman.

Her motive was twofold – first to get authority from him to alleviate the general conditions in the camp, and secondly, to obtain a pass for her to return to Bloemfontein.

Emily found the General looking quite ill, despondent, and extremely testy.

The news of the deaths of the three children had already reached him.

Pretyman explained to Emily that he could only issue her with a pass for his administrative area at De Aar.

Emily decided to proceed to Cape Town, with a different

pass issued by the General. Her plan was to see General Forestier-Walker to obtain a pass to return to Bloemfontein.

Also, she needed another truckload of relief supplies including clothing.

She hoped her visit to Cape Town would give her a chance to see the Rowntrees, who were returning to the UK on 27 March, and the ladies who were coming out to continue the Rowntrees' work.

But the sending and delivery of letters by hand had been banned by the military, except under strict censorship, so Emily was particularly eager to send home news by way of Rowntree.

Emily succeeded in obtaining a pass to return to Bloemfontein via Kimberley and Mafeking.

In an interview with Sir W F Hely Hutchinson, the recently-appointed Governor of the Cape Colony who had replaced Milner, Emily found him deeply interested and courteous.

Emily later remarked on the sympathy and kindness she had found in all the high-ranking officials and military men she had encountered – but only in private.

That was in contrast to their public attitude which, she later realised, was dictated by administrative pressures.

On 23 March 1901, the world at large began to learn of Boer starvation in the British-administered concentration camps in South Africa.

People like Emily and Rowntree must have been regarded as loose cannons by the South African administrative and military authorities. Indeed it was widely known, especially in his immediate military circles, that Lord Kitchener continually referred to Emily Hobhouse as "That Bloody Woman".

She was becoming a peaceful and humanitarian obstacle to his campaign of civilian removal and transportation.

In meeting some Cape workers being assembled for work in the camps, Emily described to them the conditions the inmates were enduring.

The potential workers had envisaged, at the worst, people sleeping on nice wooden floors. So they were aghast at the conditions described by Emily.

Whether Emily saw or spoke to Mr Rowntree prior to his departure from Cape Town for the UK on March 27 is not clear.

But it is known that she wanted to impress upon him the necessity of taking great care about what was published in the newspapers as the jingoistic press were likely to distort the facts.

One of the reasons why the newly-appointed Cape Colony Governor was approached by Emily was on behalf of General Pretyman.

The Governor had jurisdiction over the camps in Kimberley, Mafeking, and Warrenton – but before Emily's interview he didn't even know it.

Sir Walter, after getting over his surprise, promised to take an interest in the camps, and soon after Emily's final departure back to the UK there appeared to be a vast improvement in the Kimberley Camp conditions.

After spending 10 days in Cape Town, and having secured her pass as well as replenishing the refugee supplies for the women and children of the camps, Emily began her long train journey back to Bloemfontein.

The journey, lasting from Monday to the following Friday, was interspersed with overnight stops.

One such halt at the Orange River Station enabled Emily to visit the small camp there.

The inmates consisted of a half a dozen mothers, of whom two were pregnant, and 24 young children.

Being a very small group, they appeared to be reasonably cared for. Their immediate need was for clothing, especially child and baby clothes, which Emily was able to supply.

The British Intelligence officer who accompanied her to the camp was rather aloof and abrasive to her, but Emily kept her cool.

On a stopover in Kimberley, she also engaged the help of a Mr Hendrikz who helped her unload and deliver much-needed supplies, including clothing, to the camp's internees.

On collecting her mail, Emily discovered that the censorship order had been adhered to very strictly.

She secured an interview with the new Commandant, Colonel Parke, who had previously commanded the 18th Battalion of the Imperial Yeomanry.

The Colonel agreed that Emily could contact Cape Town to secure the services of a camp nurse.

But he pointed out that all available stores had been cannibalised by Lord Kitchener and he had no materials, such as sail cloth, for the camp inmates. Colonel Parke also divulged that he was expecting an influx of another 600 people, and that there were not enough tents for them.

On 6 April 1901, Emily recorded that there were more than 10,000 inmates in the Orange River Colony camps.

At Springfontein, she reported that another 1,000 people had arrived, despite inadequate tent accommodation for the 500 people who were already in the camp.

She had also received a request to visit the Kroonstadt Camp, where sickness and death rates were rising.

It was an urgent summons, as many inmates also had inadequate footwear and clothing.

The visit depended entirely upon the approval of Lord Kitchener.

On April 10, Emily visited the camp at Mafeking which was in an isolated area, approximately six miles out of town.

There were nearly 900 held in the camp and the inmates were desperately short of basics such as blankets, clothes, candles and soap.

Emily supplied what she could from her limited sources and organised a small committee of women which went some way towards encouraging self-help.

All of the committee women had lost their homes during the farm burning regime.

It was quite a novelty for the male inmates to see a committee of females working together, which, even in South African society generally, was dominated by males.

All were very impressed with the actions of Emily, who

was caring enough to offer them understanding and limited help, when the British authorities appeared to be indifferent to their needs.

Emily's journey on to Warrenton was yet another stressful experience.

At the railway station, she witnessed two trains full of refugees. Many of them were wedged into open coal wagons, and they had only minimal personal belongings.

The camp Superintendent, Mr Schutte, told Emily that he had only been able to arrange 25 tents for the 240 inmates on the way.

When Emily approached a member of the camp committee in an effort to obtain a meal for the influx of displaced persons, she was informed that it was not possible as nobody had been aware of their imminent arrival.

In any event, being on a late Saturday evening, it would have been impossible to procure kettles, utensils or fuel.

Later, in her reflections on the traumatic experience, Emily said she was distraught at witnessing the truckloads of hungry women and children having no homes, many having lost them in the farm burning and military clearance campaigns.

They were also having to cope with the loss of their animals, bellowing or baaing for non-existent fodder and water.

Upon returning to Bloemfontein after a two-and-a-half-day journey from Kimberley, she had been told harrowing stories of camp conditions in the area.

At the Bloemfontein Camp, for instance, there was a

severe problem with food supplies. With a sudden influx of a further 500 refugees, 400 were without even basic meat rations.

There was also a serious shortage of drinks, such as coffee, sugar was almost non-existent, and most inmates had to rely on coarse bread for basic sustenance.

No wonder sickness and malnutrition prevailed.

It was becoming obvious to Emily, who had been worn to distraction and weariness in her lone campaign for the unfortunate women and children, that her relief strategy should be reviewed.

She came to the conclusion that perhaps more could be achieved by returning to Britain and embarking on a public campaign to persuade the Government and members of the public to give help and support to the disease-ridden and dying Boer women and children.

In an interview with Colonel Goold-Adams, Emily cited the 20 per cent death rate in the camps.

The Colonel said he believed that a further, vast influx of forced refugees was inevitable.

On the subject of Lord Kitchener's refusal to grant Emily a permit to proceed to the camps North of Bloemfontein, Goold Adams was more forthcoming.

It was not a prudent gesture to show any sign of sympathy or social liaison with the Boers, he claimed.

There were many informants in the camps who carried tales of such liaison and help back to the military.

As some of these camps were being administered in a semi-civil and military manner, the authority looked upon anyone who was prepared to help the suffering souls as a political as well as military impediment.

This meant that even such a benevolent-minded person could be perceived as an interfering spy.

Throughout France, Switzerland, Italy and Germany, the news of the malnutrition, death from disease, farm burning, and general neglect of the mainly Boer women and children, was becoming very well known.

The British South African military authorities had managed to keep a tight lid on the situation so far, but the facts were ready to explode in the European area especially.

On Emily's final visit to the Bloemfontein Camp, she told the refugees that she believed people in Britain would be far more sympathetic and helpful if she could relate her personal experiences.

At that stage, she was not aware of the bigoted attitude of certain editors in the jingoistic press towards her ministrations of mercy.

GENERAL VISCOUNT KITCHENER
G.C.B., O.M., G.C.M.G.

Lord Kitchener as Commander-in-Chief, continued the farm
destruction policy. Additionally he instituted the
Concentration Camp arrangements.

RETURN TO THE UK

E MILY sailed for the UK from Cape Town aboard the RMS Saxon, leaving South Africa on 7 May 1901. As coincidence would have it, Sir Alfred Milner was aboard the same ship. Emily succeeded in gaining an interview with him and was quite surprised when he said he had received 60 reports of allegations of spying by Emily.

She assured him she had kept strictly to her undertaking to avoid political talk or influence and she got the impression that he believed her.

Emily ventured that, when one makes enquiries about an honourable person, one must employ honourable persons and not unreliable informers.

When Emily broached the subject of a future return to South Africa, Sir Alfred intimated via his private secretary, a Mr Walrond, that she need not bother to learn the local language of Afrikaans as she would not be permitted to return.

Sir Alfred, after his arrival, was honoured with a peerage, and became Viscount Milner.

After a holiday in the UK, he once again returned to South Africa, sailing back on 10 August 1901.

General Sir John Maxwell had distinguished himself during the South African campaign.

Initially, he had been given command of the 14th

Brigade, and was at Krantz Kraal, Zand River and again at Brandfort.

After those conflicts, Sir John had been appointed as Military Governor of Pretoria.

The General was married to Louise Maxwell, an American whose roots still lay in the United States.

Just prior to Emily's return to Britain, The New York Herald Tribune carried a letter from Lady Maxwell.

It was mainly an appeal to the American people to provide warm clothing for the Boer women and children who were living, virtually destitute, in the refugee camps.

Lady Maxwell wrote that Britain was quite exhausted due to continual funding of her own soldiers, their wives and children.

As an American, she felt that such an appeal to her sympathetic compatriots would elicit a generous response.

Lady Maxwell was moved to write her appeal after visiting some of the camps in the Transvaal.

Here was another woman in a highly sensitive social position who had been sufficiently impressed by the plight of the Boer women and children that she was motivated to do something about the situation.

In addition to having major repercussions in the United States, the letter caused great embarrassment in military and government circles, both in South Africa and the United Kingdom.

This also split public opinion. On the one hand, Lady Maxwell was accused of being pro-Boer by the jingoists, while on the other, more sympathetic people viewed her as a very brave woman. Her semi-military position, as the wife of such an important General, gave authority to what was rumoured about the plight of the Boer prisoners.

The repercussions echoed right back to Lords Roberts and Kitchener. St John Brodrick, the Conservative Secretary of State for War, in a confidential telegram to Kitchener, indicated Governmental concern about General Maxwell's wife, saying that her disclosures had given rise to claims that Boer families were being neglected by the British Government.

A tidal moment of truth had begun to lap around the feet of the home authorities.

Pressures were applied to Lady Maxwell through her husband and she was forced to compromise the theme of her New York letter in a communication to The Times on July 31 1901.

She explained that she had no intention of being contemptuous of the British Government and that her motive had been simply to appeal for warm clothing and little luxuries for the camp inmates.

Such small luxuries, she wrote, included children's clothing which had not been within the orbit of army equipment.

This would have made any person with a modicum of intelligence view the apology as a result of pressure from high places.

The British public reacted with mixed feelings. Although the letter embarrassed the Government and the generals, it did little to change the attitude of the jingoists.

During Emily's South African tour of the camps she had written numerous letters referring to the conditions being experienced by the women and children.

She wrote to her brother, Leonard, who chose not to publish the correspondence.

In the event, it turned out to be a very wise decision.

The basic reason for his decision was that drawing public attention to Emily's nauseating reports of the camp conditions might prompt the military authorities to stop further access to the camps.

On her return from South Africa, Emily stayed for a brief period with her uncle and aunt, Lord and Lady Hobhouse.

She then decided on a plan to alleviate the sufferings of the civilian casualties of the war.

In early June 1901 Emily secured an interview with the Secretary of State, St John Broderick, about the suffering in the camps.

She urged the British Government to alleviate the camp conditions and she did not withhold her feelings about the maladministration by the military and civilian authority in the camps.

Recalling the interview later, Emily said the Minister listened intently to her experiences and seemed to have altered his view as to the correct strategy of the military command in the widespread creation of the camps.

As the interview drew to a close, Broderick asked Emily for suggestions to improve the conditions.

In fact, Emily had already formulated her suggestions

and had handed in her report at the War Office in London on the very afternoon that the interview had taken place.

Emily's suggestions amounted to an entire compendium of problems, which included: Lack of beds, mattresses, fuel, soap, and the monotonous and unsuitable diet; insufficient and insanitary water supplies for general hygiene, especially clothes washing; overcrowding in tents and tent spacing, making privacy impossible; urgent need of blankets, clothes and footwear to insulate the camp inmates from the severe night coldness; warm clothing; adequate sanitary and toilet arrangements to dispel the terrible and offensive stench of effluvia in some camps, such as Bloemfontein, which pervaded the accommodation in a constant, degrading manner, resulting in severe throat infections; there was also a need for properly staffed hospitals, as well as educational provision for the camp children.

Even scanning this synopsis leaves you wondering at the lack of humanitarian consideration for the inmates.

Emily was further exasperated to discover later that this part of her report was misplaced in the Government files.

However, her requests had been communicated to the Committee of the Distress Fund For South African Women And Children, published by Emily Hobhouse and named "The Report".

The publication was evidently for public information also as it could be purchased in pamphlet form at the price of a penny a copy.

On the day the Committee decided to publish, Emily had written to Lord Milner advising him of their decision.

And despite her experience in Liskeard, Emily decided to attend public meetings to tell people first-hand about the camp conditions.

Throughout June and July of 1901, Emily visited London, Manchester, Bristol, Birmingham and York and many other cities.

On June 10 Emily spoke at a private meeting, mainly to influential women.

One, a Mrs Humphrey Ward, after closely questioning Emily, decided to organise another fund for camp relief work but upon discovering that the women of the Victoria League were also responding, decided to amalgamate with them.

On June 17 1901, the Liberal MP David Lloyd George sought an adjournment debate in the House on the conditions of the detention camps in South Africa and the alarming rate of mortality among the women and children detained there.

He said that for the good name of this country, something should be done.

He also asked why the children were being punished, and he requested that the debate should have a non-political profile.

His proposal was seconded by John Ellis, who also requested that accredited persons be sent to report on these camps.

The main contender during the debate appeared to be St John Broderick.

He complained that he had been furnished with no prior

notice of the debate, and he refused to accept that it should be a non-political discussion.

He presumably felt the need for the mantle of a political majority to parry any major criticism of himself.

But Broderick did, for the first time, quote statistics stating that 250,000 troops had to be fed prior to the needs of 63,000 refugees.

Sir Henry Campbell Bannerman, the Liberal leader of the Opposition, replied that if formal notice of the motion had been given, any attempt at a debate would have been blocked by the Government.

Although Emily was not personally named, it was quite obvious that she had succeeded in focussing the glare of publicity on Westminster.

The effects of the publicity resulting from the Hobhouse revelation, which was still within the socio-humanitarian orbit, had spilled over into the political arena.

It was inevitable as it was impossible to separate the two.

Emily had been forced to approach various politicians in her effort to publicise the plight of the camp inmates.

One approach had been to Campbell-Bannerman, who was like a rider straddling two horses.

On the right side of the divide were the Liberal Imperialists, such as H H Asquith, Richard Haldane and Sir Edward Grey.

On the left side of this party were the members described as pro-Boers, including the eloquent debater and radical, Lloyd George, with Sir William Harcourt and John Morley.

At the outset of the South African War, Campbell-Bannerman had supported the policies of the Tory Government in power.

His leaning had been the result of a patriotic conviction; the air of humanity in the conduct of the war at that moment did not enter the equation of the war's progression.

Emily's interview with Campbell-Bannerman had lasted for almost two hours.

He listened intently to her harrowing stories of farm burning, destruction of crops and cattle, mass deportation and detention, semi-starvation, fever, disease and multiple deaths of women and children.

As she told of the indifferent attitude of many officials, and the alarming way in which the circumstances were being viewed by European nations, Sir Henry was an intent and deeply moved listener.

Being given first-hand knowledge of the true conditions of the Boer internees, Sir Henry altered his already faltering point of view.

The meeting took place a few days after Emily's interview with St John Broderick.

On the very evening of Emily's interview with Campbell -Bannerman, he appeared with Sir William Harcourt as guests at a banquet given by the National Reform Union at the Holborn Restaurant in London in their honour.

On 15 June 1901, The Times published a report of the speeches of the two honoured guests.

One of the initial points reported in Campbell-

Bannerman's speech queried the Government policy of having got the men Britain had been fighting against, down.

Why, he asked, should we continue to punish them so severely, by devastating their country, continuing to burn their homes, break up their very instruments of agriculture, and destroying the machinery by which food was produced?

Sweeping the destitute women and children into camps, where they were devoid of all the decencies, comforts and many of the necessities of life, had resulted in a death rate of 430 in 1,000 in some of the camps.

On the previous day, he had asked the Leader of the House of Commons when the information would be afforded, of which they were so sadly in want, but his request had been refused.

Mr Balfour treated them to a short disquisition on the nature of the war.

Campbell-Bannerman continued by quoting the phrase "War is war", but when one came to ask about it, one was told that no war was going on – that it was not a war (Laughter).

When was a war not a war? (Laughter).

When it was carried on by methods of barbarism in South Africa (Cheers).

Then Mr Balfour went on to give an account of numbers and made out there were 17,000 in the field against Britain.

A good many things had been scattered in the last year.

Prudence, justice, common sense and consistency had gone and now the venerable science of arithmetic appeared to have gone by the board also.

When the war began, we were told that there were 30,000 burghers who could come into the field against us, he continued.

Since then, a great many have been killed or incapacitated through wounds and disease, some 17,000 had been deported, and we never opened a newspaper without seeing that another score or two had been made prisoners; and yet 17,000 still remained in the field out of the 30,000 (Laughter).

Campbell Bannerman then proceeded to complain about the conduct of the Home and Colonial administration. One of his final remarks was that British colonies throughout the world were held without difficulty in loyal friendship to us.

Why? Because we treated them as equals.

The sentiment of the Boers to us, as a result of the policy pursued, would not only be that of racial jealousy, and of political antipathy; it would be a personal hatred and a sense – an ineradicable sense – of personal wrong. ("Hear hear.")

In conclusion, Campbell-Bannerman said he hoped that, by some means, the Government would be compelled to obtain information on all those matters and to give it to the people; and he was altogether mistaken in the character of his countrymen, and still more of his country women if, when they realised the facts, they did not instantly demand the adoption of some wholly different method to that hitherto pursued of arriving at that settlement which it was the desire of us all to achieve (Cheers).

Sir William Harcourt stated in supporting him, that he was glad "to hold the hoe to him".

Sir William then proceeded to relate the root of the problem as being a subsidised insurrection – an armed invasion of the South African Republic organised by the Prime Minister of the Cape Colony (Cecil Rhodes), a Privy Councillor of the Queen, with his confederates, the gold gamblers of the Rand, who had been made heroes.

Talking of the Boers, he said: "In the War Press it seems a patriotic thing to represent them in the worst character."

He concluded with a warning that the gold speculators were the principal authors of the war, and that there was a possibility of a native insurrection to follow.

Such public statements as rendered by those pillars of society, although highlighting statistical flaws in Government statements, encouraged outbursts of sentiment, echoed through the national press.

Emily's report achieved major national coverage on 19 June 1901 in The Daily News.

On the same day, The Times, in quoting excerpts from Emily's pamphlet, stated that, although Emily had described some painful sights that she had witnessed, and painful tales that she had heard, the newspaper accused her of accepting it without much investigation.

The Times, with Conservative sympathies, had failed to appreciate the many harrowing personal experiences witnessed by Emily. This conveyed to the general public that she was a rumour-carrying alarmist, which was far from the truth.

The editorial was an attempted smokescreen to shield the Government in power.

Certain publications even went as far as to lampoon Emily, despite her efforts at trying to gain public sympathy and help for the diseased and dying women and children.

One such indelicate example was published in the satirical magazine Punch on 3 July 1901.

Headed British Brutality, the article contained the following:

With regard to the outcry recently raised by Miss Hobhouse, and others, against the conditions of the Boer Refugee Camps for women and children.

Mr Punch 's Lady Commissions, having made exhaustive enquiries, now reports as follows:

I. The supply of hairpins is wholly inadequate.

2. The whole camp of 573 women had but one back number of a Ladies paper amongst them, with a fashion plate depicting a positively odious costume of last season.

3. Only five bottles of Violettes de Parms scent to be found throughout.

4. No spirit lamps for the proper heating of curling tongs – this is a fact.

5. Owing to their military duties, none of the British Officers ever come into afternoon tea with, or do anything to socially entertain, the Boer ladies.

This is looked upon as particularly brutal conduct and makes one quite inclined to believe in almost any charge of neglect.

Undaunted, Emily continued to attend various meetings. At the Bristol Redland Park Hall, at a meeting chaired by Joseph Fry, Emily received an encouraging report from the Bristol Mercury on July 10, despite being interrupted by a gang described as hobbledehoys by a William Pepler who had attended.

Two days earlier, her meeting at the Congregational Church Hall in New Southgate was described in the Daily News as boisterous.

One member of the opposition even wore a Union Jack flag as a bib.

Despite such disturbances, Emily's message remained an embarrassment to the Government.

THE COMMITTEE OF
LADY VISITORS

—————▷◦◁—————

O
N 22 July 1901, St John Broderick announced the formation of a Committee Of Lady Visitors to attend and report on the Boer Concentration Camps. Their brief was also to co-operate with local committees. At last, Government action and public awareness of the refugee and concentration camp situation in South Africa was a reality.

The leader of the group of women visitors was the well-known Liberal National Imperialist, Milicent Fawcett.

She had earlier been elected President of the National Union of Women's Suffrage Societies.

And as a leader of the new all-female committee, she had broken new ground as it was the first non-male group ever to be officially appointed.

Although both women had the suffragette movement at heart, there their common interests ended, as Milicent Fawcett had pro-Government imperialist sympathies.

For example, she supported the "No taxation without representation" demand of the Uitlanders.

This was in line with her own sentiments over votes for women. In her sympathetic leaning toward the cry of the Uitlanders, many felt that she was possibly unsympathetic towards the Boer refugees.

The remainder of the women's committee included Lady Knox, who had previously helped nurse the sick and wounded at Ladysmith; Miss Lucy Deane, experienced in enquiries dealing with women and children in factories; Dr Ella Scarlett and Dr Jane Waterston, both at that time in South Africa; and a Miss Brereton, also in South Africa, who had supervised one of the Yeomanry hospitals, set up by an organisation of women in the UK under the patronage of Lady Curzon.

Some of the women had already indicated a bias against Emily Hobhouse and her supporters, and became known as the "Whitewashing Commission", though it was felt by many others to be an unfair title.

Although it was felt that most of the women had a close governmental affiliation, they did generally uphold Emily's findings and made the appropriate recommendations to the British Government for improvements and alleviation of suffering within the camps.

Expenses were to be paid to the women pro rata, which, apart from travelling, were to be four guineas per person per day, and one guinea a day for an accompanying servant, plus a £100 outfit allowance.

Their mode of transport was also a world apart from that experienced by Emily Hobhouse.

She observed that in addition to having their own coach on the train they travelled on, with associated sleeping and saloon accommodation, they had their own kitchen and staff of one cook, two saloon attendants, and a boy servant.

Permits for camp entry were easily accessible, and as they

were able to sleep on the train, there was no need for hotel or boarding house arrangements.

Emily had received a certain amount of adverse comments and publicity from various newspapers in both editorials and reports.

Other published comments commended her enlightened cause in the face of such jingoistic opposition.

One such supportive contribution was contained in a letter published in the Manchester Guardian on 5 August 1901.

The author was a very distinguished Field Marshal, a military officer of the highest rank, who had served with distinction in the Afghan and Indian campaigns.

Field Marshal Sir Neville Chamberlain's letter is worthy of quotation:

Sir, In a speech lately delivered by Sir Edward Grey at Peterborough, he expressed the opinion that there must be room for free speech, and that free speech on one side was provocative of free speech on the other.

On that equitable basis, I, as a Liberal, feel bound to differ with the conclusion drawn by Sir Edward, that the war in South Africa has been conducted throughout in accordance with the accepted rules of civilised warfare. I dissent because the necessity has never been made clear to the nation to justify a departure from the recognised laws of international warfare.

I mean the frequent injudicious, if not reckless, burning or sacking of the farmsteads or homes of the Boers, the removal or destruction of the food stored in their houses for the maintenance of their families, the sweeping away of all cattle and sheep, the destruction of mills and implements of agriculture, as also the forcible removal into camps of all women and children, and their being kept in bondage.

I do not wish to imply that extreme measures are never justified during war, but I do assert that the daily reports which have appeared in the press during the past seven or eight months indicate that a great wave of destruction has been spread over the Orange and Vaal States, such as has never before been enacted by our armies; in fact, to use a significant Kaffir expression, they have been, and are continued to be, subjected to the process of being 'eaten up'.

No doubt, instances of violence and cruelty have often disgraced the military operations of all European Powers, but whenever they have occurred they have taken place in violation of the laws of international warfare.

In times past, British generals have earned an honourable repute for moderation and humanity in their dealings with the people of the country in which they have had to operate, and the history of our nation tells us that war can be carried on with safety to the troops and, with brilliant success without resorting to methods of oppression, and the more especially against the families of the combatants and non-combatants.

Even in the dark days of the Indian Mutiny, when there was an ever-present sense of the inhumanities practised by the mutineers and others who abetted them, there never existed the idea that the horrors of war were to be indiscriminately carried into the homes of the population.

Happily the representative of the Crown, then in India, was a nobleman of calm, humane instincts, and history now lauds the part played by the man, who at the time, was railed against as 'Clemency Canning'.

The conditions and the suffering of which Miss Hobhouse assures us she was a witness ought to be enough to make it impossible for them ever to be repeated.

It surely can never become a recognised episode in war for wives to be forcibly torn from their homes and to know not what had become of their children; for women about to become mothers, to be forced into railway trucks, and to have to travel tedious journeys, and then to remain in camps devoid of the comforts needed for maternity; for women and children to be sent to live in bare tents, and often exposed to sleeping on the wet ground or to be drenched under leaky tents, or for mothers to see their little ones dwindle and die, for the want of suitable nourishment.

Such have been the events that Miss Hobhouse states to have taken place, and the order which brought them about was planned, and carried out, with culpable disregard of such results…

It is true that the nation has been lately assured by the Government, and by its generals in command of the forces in South Africa, that for the safety of our troops, and to enable the war to be carried on, all the measures to which I take exception are indispensable.

In a word, the justification set forth by the authorities, is that the end justifies the means.

If that dogma be a just one, and it is to hold good in all the wars that are to take place in the future, then indeed the doctrines and practices enjoined by the Christian religion must be held to possess no jurisdiction over the sphere of politics of war.

One of the aspersions cast in the face of the Boers, is that they are now carrying on a Guerilla warfare.

Can the measures I have especially referred to, come under any other heading? It would seem to have passed out of mind that the Boers in arms have never ceased to possess the rights of belligerents.

They are still brave patriots fighting for independence...

It is said that coming events often cast their shadows before them.

This was certainly the case so far back at the time, when Bloemfontein was first occupied, for the spirit then beginning to be evinced in certain quarters led me to say, in a letter I wrote to a relative at that place, that it seemed to me that before the war was ended, the Government might find itself in the position of having to feed the Boer population as well as its own army.

Sir Neville, as a Brigadier General, had been in command of a mobile column in the Indian Mutiny of 1857, and the then Lieut Roberts (later Field Marshal Lord Roberts) was his Staff Officer.

Field Marshal Chamberlain was called "Coeur de Lion"

by Sir Charles Napier, who also described him as "the very soul of Chivalry".

The Ladies' Commission Report, finalised in December 1901, did much to confirm the initial findings and public complaints that originated from Emily Hobhouse.

As a result, many of the camp reports remained confidential when referred back to the Government authorities.

One of the most neglected camps mentioned was at Mafeking.

A medical report from the camp dated October 1 1901 revealed that of the 2,500 children under 12 in the camp, 381 had died during the month.

By November 1, children under 12 numbered 2,088, and 149 had died prior to the 21st day of the month.

This did not include very young babies only a few days old, or non-white children.

The Medical Officer excused this situation on the grounds that already-infected persons (as far as he knew) had been introduced into the camp. He also cited what he described as the sanitary ignorance of the camp inmates; their want of personal cleanliness, unwillingness to ventilate tents, inter-visiting, thereby overcrowding the tents; and improper use of Dutch medicines.

This whitewash of the facts is in contrast to the Ladies' Commission recommendations dated 11 November 1901, which read as follows:

1. Boilers sufficient to boil all drinking water should be supplied to all the camps.

2. Public bake ovens be supplied to all camps.

3. A ration of vegetables or lime juice to be added once weekly to existing rations.

4. That from April, fat dripping or lard should be added to the diet of the internees.

5. A supervisory water engineer visit the camps to advise and make efficient use of individual camp water supply.

6. Requirement of Home Government to send out at least 100 trained British teachers. Requested in August, no reaction to date.

7. Instruct every camp Superintendent to be more liberal with existing stringent fuel supplies.

8. Appoint camp Matrons as soon as suitable persons are found.

9. As soon as possible, supplement supply of foodstuffs on sale in camp stores. Particularly urgent at camps Vredefort Road and Heilbron, shops there bare of food.

10. Major disorganisation at Brandfort Hospital, immediate attention and action required. A competent Medical Officer of repute to be sent to make a special report. While the present severe sickness lasts, all possible help should be given to Brandfort by way of supply of nurses and doctors.

A comparison of the previous Hobhouse reports and recommendations on the camp conditions supports her findings, and points to the inaction of the Government administrators and Army authorities.

It is important to note that although the public saw Milicent Fawcett as the woman facilitating the concentration camp improvements, that was not the case. Without a shadow of doubt, Fawcett is deserving of praise which was rewarded by public recognition.

But the true architect, pioneer and heroine in her struggle through a jungle of male chauvinist and jingoistic opposition was the indomitable Emily Hobhouse.

The senior administrators' reaction to these reports and recommendations was a humanitarian series of measures for the relief of the camp inmates.

Sir Alfred Milner, in a memo to General Maxwell and Colonel Goold-Adams, dated 20 November 1901, stated that the Government would shrink from no measures, however costly, to mitigate the evil of the camps.

He also stated that he was under the impression that the practice of a further overwhelming influx of refugees into the camps, must soon be ended.

In a Colonial Office memorandum to the Home Government on 6 December 1901, Lord Kitchener indignantly and entirely denied the accusations of cruelty and rough treatment of women and children brought in from their farms to the camps.

He added that hardships had previously been inseparable from this process, but the Boer women themselves bore testimony to the kindness and consideration shown by our soldiers on all occasions.

This letter was in response to a complaint written on 21 November 1901 by Schalk Burgher, acting State President of the Transvaal, to Lord Salisbury.

"The Boer President requested that his own commission

into the state of the camps, health wise, be facilitated," he wrote.

The proposed inspection by the Boers could have had significant propaganda value, so the request was declined by the Home Government.

It had, during the latter quarter of the year of 1901, been a period of turbulence in political and military circles for Great Britain.

On October 10, General Buller was relieved of his command for, it was stated, "indiscretion and lack of military discipline".

During the same month in Edinburgh, the Colonial Secretary, Joseph Chamberlain, embarked on an anti-German speech in defence of the Boer camps.

In November the leader of the Liberal opposition, Sir Henry Campbell-Bannerman, condemned the extension of martial law to Cape Town and the other major South African ports.

On November 15 1901, in an official report published in London, it was admitted that the death rate in the camps, especially among children, was still rising.

It also stated that urgent action was under way to alleviate and improve camp conditions.

Partial blame was then accorded to the internees themselves. It was claimed that the Boer mothers were treating their children's measles with a tea made up of goat's dung.

The report also alleged that the Boers suffered through their insanitary habits, with deplorable consequences.

In quoting statistics, the report stated that in addition to the 77,000 whites in the Orange River and Transvaal camps, there were approximately 21,000 non-whites, mostly servants and farm workers of the Boers.

The report concluded by stating that while supporting many allegations, it refuted charges in the continental press of deliberate neglect and brutality.

The final statement claimed that the Boers' mortality rate was often just as high on their farms.

This latter claim did not stand up to close analysis, as there was no serious overcrowding in the Boer farmsteads.

As a concluding episode to this closing period of 1901, it was reported in London that Anglo-German talks with reference to a possible alliance were suspended (December 19), following Joseph Chamberlain's anti-German remarks.

Having attended some 40 public meetings which, with three exceptions, were peaceful and orderly, Emily had generally received mixed reactions.

Some of her more extreme critics described her as a political agitator, a disseminator of inaccurate and blood-curdling stories.

She was even accused of being a vehicle for transmitting political propaganda.

Further support for Emily's mission, apart from that of many close friends and acquaintances, came from Sir Neville Chamberlain.

In another letter to the Manchester Guardian, dated 29 August 1901, the Field Marshall once again cited the wholesale reckless destruction and abduction of families enacted by the British Army, with the approval of the

British Government. He also pointed out that the mortality figures indicated that 10 women and children were dying in South Africa for every one in London.

Deported!

———※-●-※———

TOWARDS the end of 1901, Emily Hobhouse made plans to return to South Africa. There were a host of reasons that prompted her return to bring further help to the camp inmates. One consideration was to help a large number of deportees who were awaiting trans-shipment in many coastal towns such as Cape Town, Durban, East London and Port Elizabeth.

Many of them were destitute. Additionally, Emily had been urged to take up the cause on behalf of the British refugees, and she was ready to do so.

Emily had a long discussion with Lord Ripon on her relief strategies.

She was given a letter of introduction by Lady Ripon to Lady Hely-Hutchinson, wife of the Governor of Cape Colony, Sir Walter Hely Hutchinson.

Emily booked a berth for herself and an experienced young nurse, Elizabeth Philips, on the SS Avondale Castle, due to sail for Cape Town on October 5 1901.

Although destined for work in the camps, Elizabeth had been recommended as a companion for Emily by Canon Barnett to help alleviate the monotony of the relatively slow journey.

Emily told the shipping line that she required anonymity throughout the journey, and that her name was not to be included on the passenger list. She was aware that any further visit to the camps by her could be prohibited by the military authority, especially now that martial law was due to be declared at all Cape Ports.

It was enacted by Sir Gordon Sprigg, Prime Minister of the Cape Colony, on October 9 1901.

Despite Emily's request for anonymity, word of her departure leaked out.

She had become very well known publicly during her meetings. It had been said that an intended passenger for South Africa, a keen-eyed journalist, had become aware of her boarding the ship and reported, possibly quite erroneously, that Emily intended to revisit the camps.

Although the intention was incorrectly reported it was known that Emily had become concerned and alarmed at the imperceptible progress with which the Ladies' Commission's recommendations were being expedited by the civil and military authorities in the concentration camps.

News of Emily's intended visit rapidly reached the Colonial Office, then it went via Joseph Chamberlain to Cape Town where Lord Milner and General Kitchener received the despatch.

Realising the potential of the arrival of this "important critic of the Camp conditions", Lord Kitchener acted immediately.

Using the recent declaration of martial law, Kitchener decided that Emily would not be permitted to enter South Africa.

Enforcement of his decision was delegated to the administrative Commander, Major General A S Wynne, then to the Commander of the Base, Colonel H Cooper, who, in turn, delegated the execution of the order to a less senior officer.

At this juncture, it is of interest to consider some of the conditions that were required under martial law.

The agreement stipulated that the military authorities should leave the control of the harbour, docks and railways in the hands of the civil authorities, and should not interfere with the ordinary course of business, or the liberty of well-behaved persons.

The military were to exercise control over the landing and departure of undesirables, and had the power to deport persons who were not British subjects.

They might censor letters, and messages, but only with the object of preventing intelligence reaching the enemy, etc.

The law also stated that no commandeering of goods and animals was to be permitted in the newly-proclaimed areas, and British subjects were not to be arrested, by order of the military authorities, save upon an affidavit charging them with the commission of a crime, and upon the certificate of the Attorney-General that such an affidavit justified the arrest.

In the light of this, it is patently obvious that Lord Kitchener, Major General Wynne, Colonel Hooper and subordinate officers grossly ignored the provisions of the law when they barred and deported the newly-arrived

Emily from Cape Town, bearing in mind that she was a British Citizen.

Her ship had arrived on Sunday October 27 1901. On anchoring offshore, the passengers were awaiting the arrival of the passenger tender alongside for their disembarkation.

When it arrived, there were military personnel on its upper deck who boarded the passenger ship.

In the smoking lounge every passenger was interviewed by a naval officer.

After Emily's interview by a Lieutenant Lingham she was sent to the end of the queue.

Later, in the presence of the ship's Captain, in his cabin, the Lieutenant informed Emily that she was under arrest.

Lieutenant Lingham told the Captain that Emily should not be permitted to land anywhere in South Africa, and no communication was to be allowed by Emily in writing or speech with anyone ashore.

He then gave Emily the option of remaining where she was, or returning to the UK on the following Wednesday on the RMS Carisbrooke Castle.

The Lieutenant said he would return the following day but just prior to leaving, again warned Emily that she was forbidden to communicate with anyone on shore, either by word of mouth or in writing.

Emily was now a prisoner. She had just completed a long turbulent voyage, through the notorious Bay of Biscay, and on down the exposed West African coastline.

Furthermore, she was to experience extended imprisonment aboard a ship that was due to dock alongside the

South Arm jetty. This was necessary for the disembarkation and reprovisioning of stores and the dirty, dust-infiltrating requirement to "coal ship", truly a nauseous experience.

All this imposition upon Emily would have delighted General Kitchener, who was known to have been very angry at "That Bloody Woman".

After Lieutenant Lingham left the ship, Emily proceeded to write some letters, all in the same vein of her previous complaints.

The letters, addressed to Milner, Kitchener, Hely-Hutchinson and Colonel Cooper, alleged that the purpose of her visit was non-political and purely charitable. She re-stated her wish to assist British refugees, whom she understood were impoverished in some of the coastal towns.

She also said her health was not robust enough to stand the strain of being a shipboard prisoner.

Emily requested that she be allowed to stay ashore with friends for a brief period.

She also requested that her nurse, Miss Philips, be allowed to land.

The latter request was the only one that was finally acceded to.

Lieutenant Lingham had promised Emily that her letters to senior officials would be forwarded.

Her letters complained repeatedly about the "arrest of an Englishwoman, intending to do works of a charitable and philanthropical nature", without an official warrant of any kind or written accusation of any offence committed by her.

The following day, Lieutenant Lingham returned aboard and took Emily's four letters for delivery.

It would appear that Colonel Cooper and Lieutenant Lingham had begun a correspondence about Emily.

Whether this was a strategy by Colonel Cooper to remain remote from the woman prisoner is not clear.

Emily had requested in her letter to Colonel Cooper that he should inform her, in writing, of the exact regulations to which he required her to conform, whilst being held a prisoner, aboard Avondale Castle.

In a further letter from the Colonel to Lieutenant Lingham, dated October 30 1901, he said that in view of Emily's inability to leave the ship while alongside, due to the rough outgoing passage, and not being well, he had decided to place her on another ship.

On October 31, Cooper again wrote to Lingham with the news that the General Officer Commanding Cape Colony (Major General Wynne) had received a telegram from Lord Kitchener.

This telegram was from Pretoria, dated October 29 1901, stating that he and the High Commissioner (Lord Milner), had agreed not to permit Miss Hobhouse to disembark.

The letter from the Colonel instructed Lieutenant Lingham to inform Emily to be prepared at short notice for transfer to another ship returning to the United Kingdom.

Emily, upon receiving the message and instructions, wrote once again to Colonel Cooper, advising him that she remained unwell, and that it was quite impossible for her to even contemplate an early passage back to the United Kingdom.

October 31 1901 proved to be decisive both for the military authority and Emily.

The Captain of the Avondale Castle, Captain Brown, was looked upon by Emily as a friend who sympathised with her plight.

Emily reflected on the experience of another of her ancestors, Bishop Trelawny, who was held prisoner in the Tower of London in 1688.

Reinforced by the thought, Emily decided to refuse to contribute toward her keep while imprisoned on board ship.

She also decided that the cost of her homeward passage should rest with the Government and not her.

Passive resistance was, she felt, the only way she could effectively protest.

Colonel Williamson, an army doctor, sent Emily his visiting card, which she refused to accept, and she also declined to be seen by him.

One of Emily's shoreside friends, Betty Molteno, was also present and gave us an account of what happened.

After her refusal to see him, Colonel Williamson concluded that Emily was "quite fit to return to England at once!".

Two army nurses, Sisters Mackillan and Nicholson, appeared one each side of Emily with instructions to take her.

When Emily asked the nurses to take their hands off her,

they answered that they were under military orders. Emily replied that the laws of humanity and nature were higher than military laws, and appealed to them not to sully their sacred office as nurses by accosting a sick woman.

Both sisters then left the room in silence without molesting Emily, who thanked them.

Upon the return of Williamson, Emily requested that she be examined by her own physician, Dr Charles Murray.

Colonel Williamson retorted that he would not permit it, and that Dr Murray would not get a pass.

When Lingham reported that the two nursing sisters were unable to persuade Emily to move, Colonel Williamson informed Emily that if she continued to be obstructive, he had orders from the Base Commander, Colonel Cooper, to remove her by force.

Lieutenant Lingham said he had been to the RMS Roslin Castle and explained the position to the Officer Commanding troops, who had men sent to the Avondale Castle at once.

Betty Molteno said she had asked Colonel Williamson if he could not do something, as Emily was physically not in a fit state to travel.

The Colonel replied that, being under the direct orders of Lord Kitchener, he had to enforce them, and deportation of Emily must proceed.

A while later, a stretcher party arrived on the scene.

Colonel Williamson tried to persuade Emily to go quietly, but she replied that the actions being taken against her were not even within the orbit of martial law and that he had no right to interfere with private individuals. The Colonel replied that he was not there to argue and he signalled to the men to proceed.

As they attempted to lift the struggling Emily through the smoke room cabin doorway, the Colonel told them: "Be careful, don't hurt the lady."

Outside the smoking room, more soldiers were waiting, and Emily was lifted and carried, still strongly objecting, off the ship and on to the dockside.

She was then escorted, with her possessions, to the Roslin Castle, where she was forcibly carried up the gangway.

Her arrest and deportation received wide publicity, and there was a considerable reaction in the United Kingdom.

The Roslin Castle, with her prisoner passenger, sailed for England on November 1 1901.

The deportation was reported in great detail in the national press, and interest grew after Emily arrived safely at Southampton on November 24 1901.

An article in The Daily News of November 25 1901 was headlined "The return of Miss Hobhouse… A deported prisoner… The story of her first mission… Why she is punished… A campaign against a woman."

The article described Emily as having returned as a deported prisoner from South Africa and it then referred to her family pedigree.

Two of her cousins, Charles and Henry Hobhouse, were Members of Parliament, and another, The Reverend Walter Hobhouse, was editor of The Guardian.

Her uncle, Lord Hobhouse, was a Privy Councillor, another uncle was a retired Colonial Bishop, and her brother Leonard was described as the well-known Oxford philosopher and writer.

The article said that few families had such a distinguished record in so many branches of life.

Some members of society regarded it as their greatest distinction that they had produced a woman who had vindicated the humanity of Englishwomen, inspiring Godly fear into the minds of Government.

This article then proceeded to dismember her critics in their misrepresentation of Emily as hysterical, a pro-Boer, and a political propagandist.

Most significantly, it said: "Never before in British history has the whole machinery of Empire been brought to bear against a single unprotected woman."

The extended report concluded with two final observations, the first referring to "Murder To The Children". It said that the men who had been sent to look after the children were part of the system that killed them.

Emily had condemned it, and that had earned her the hostility of the Government.

In the concluding paragraph of this article, headed "The Unpardonable Sin", the newspaper pointed out that Emily had simply stated the truth, which was just what the Government wanted to avoid.

For that, she had never been forgiven, and the Government's response was to impose a series of punishments upon her, of which deportation was merely the last act.

THE PRISONER RETURNS

—➤•◄—

EMILY was met off the ship by Leonard Courtney and his wife, Kate, and her old friend, Dorothy Bradby. Emily then travelled to London to stay with her aunt and uncle in Bruton Street.

Messages of sympathy poured in for Emily from all over Britain and elsewhere and she was invited to speak at private and public functions.

But she felt quite unable to respond because her recent experiences had left her debilitated and exhausted.

Her aunt's doctor insisted that to restore her health, she had to have a complete rest.

Despite all the support she was receiving, there were far more people interested in the victorious outcome of the war than there were pacifists and objectors to it.

Some very powerful criticisms of Emily began to appear in the national press.

The Times had for quite some time published critical and sometimes scathing reports on Emily and her peaceful humanitarianism.

An editorial, published on January 24 1902, complained that Emily, after her first visit to South Africa, had appended to a somewhat hysterical account of the Boer camps a number of personal reports, accusing her fellow countrymen of cruelty and brutality.

The article then asked why should she imagine the highest military and civil officials in South Africa and at home should have been compelled to give their attention to her self-made grievances.

Earlier, on December 5 1901, it had been reported in the press that her uncle, Lord Hobhouse, had instructed the legal attorneys Lewis & Lewis to test the legality of Emily's compulsory confinement and consider an action for false imprisonment and assault.

The day before the Times editorial appeared, Lord Hobhouse authorised the Press Association to go public with an account of the correspondence between Emily's attorneys and the War Office.

It had been very evasive on matters of constitutional law and further points, such as who could be held responsible for the acts complained of.

It was obvious that identifying the defendant or defendants was fraught with serious doubts and difficulties.

Could the blame be appended to the owners of the Avondale Castle, the Union Castle Line, or to the Captain of the ship on which Emily was held? Could the two nursing sisters, the escort soldiers, or Lieutenant Lingham be responsible?

Did the responsibility rest with Colonel Cooper or with Colonel Williamson, who had made a medical and psychological assessment of Emily that would have further implications in any dispute. Or could the blame be placed on the heads of Lords Kitchener, or Milner, who had delegated the problem to the others?

And finally, did the ultimate blame fall upon Joseph Chamberlain, or the Prime Minister of the Home Government?

The legal wrangle continued until, in February 1902, Emily and Lord Hobhouse received the disappointing news that it would no longer be prudent to proceed with the case.

Five eminent Counsel stated their collective opinion that, in view of a certain passage of an Act of Indemnity, the legal action would be defeated.

The leading Counsel, Arthur Cohen, waived his fee and said later in a letter to Emily that he felt strongly that the authorities had committed an outrage upon her, in a stupid and offensive manner.

But he concluded that upon further reflection, the advice he had given was sound and right.

So ended Emily's hopes of legal redress.

Her health had not improved despite the period of rest she semi-enjoyed after her dramatic deportation.

Meanwhile, letters of support and criticism continued to be forwarded to her.

In February 1902, she was guest of honour at a dinner at the new Reform Club.

She had been invited by C P Scott, the editor of The Manchester Guardian.

It was the first time a woman had been honoured at such a prestigious evening.

As a gesture of goodwill and esteem, it was in marked contrast to the general diffidence and scepticism displayed by the jingoistic press. Having been jubilant that Emily had been removed from South Africa, some newspapers still insisted that she was an alarmist.

The Suffering of The Blacks

⟢—◈—⟢

L ITTLE has ever been known, due to official secrecy, of the conditions and suffering that internees had been exposed to in what were termed the black or native camps. Emily referred from time to time, during her initial visit, to some of the camps and, in her references to the imprisoned native population of the camps, Emily reported the following:

Unable myself, from lack of time and strength, to investigate the conditions or personally carry relief to the native camps, I confidently expected that the Ladies' Commission would have made it a part of their work to do so.

After the issue of their Report, which showed that they had not touched this important branch of the concentration system, l called upon Mr Fox Bourne, and laid before him facts which had come to my knowledge when in South Africa.

Clergymen, who worked among the coloured people in these camps, and others, told me sad tales of the sickness and mortality, which was then very high. Beyond giving a little relief for the sick, l was not able to do anything.

Subsequently Mr Fox Bourne addressed the following letter to Mr Chamberlain, whose reply is appended.
The mortality list, compiled from official sources,is obvi-

ously incomplete, and only commences in June. To my knowledge, deaths had been numerous during the previous months.

Mr Fox Bourne to Mr Chamberlain:

Sir, – I have the honour, by the direction of the Aborigines Protection Society, to address you with reference to the native refuge camps in South Africa.

From the very scanty information as to these camps which is incidentally furnished in the papers relating to the working of the refuge camps which have been laid before Parliament, it appears that, in addition to the white refugees, there were under Government control, in August 1901, 32,272 coloured persons, about five-sixths of whom were women and children, and all but about a sixteenth in the Orange River Colony; and that number had risen to 43,594 in the Orange River Colony alone on 15th November last, with which date the information as regards that Colony ceases. It further appears that the death rate in the Orange River Colony native camps, which according to the returns, was about 170 per 1,000 in August, and about 91 per 1,000 in September, rose from 137 per 1,000 in the first fortnight of October to 363 per 1,000 in the first fortnight of November.

In the Transvaal, moreover, it is shown by the returns that the number of natives in the refugee camps had risen from 1,829 in August to 39,323 in November, the latest month accounted for, and the death-rate, which was about 242 per 1,000 in August, exceeded 291 in November. If statements that have reached our Committee from private sources are accurate, the death rate at some of the native camps, including those at Bloemfontein, Edenburg, Springfontein and at Klerksdorp, greatly exceeds those appalling figures; and though the diet appointed and paid for by the authorities may be adequate, the actual supply of food is often very unsatisfactory, especially in the case of young children.

Our Committee is aware that the conditions of native life inevitably under the concentration of large numbers within limited areas are extremely insanitary, and it offers no opinion as to the policy of thus disposing of the wives and children of male natives employed for the most part in services connected with the war. But it asks that such enquiries may be instituted by His Majesty's Government as should secure for the natives who are detained no less care and humanity than are now prescribed for the Boer refuge camps.

As a preliminary to any further steps that may be deemed proper, I am to suggest the expediency of a report being called for, giving much fuller information as to the condition of these camps, the accommodation and treatment provided in each, and other details, than are contained in the Parliamentary papers; also to ask that this information, while including references to the earlier state of affairs in the Transvaal, Cape Colony, and Natal, as well as the Orange River Colony, shall be continued for the period subsequent to November, when the increased death rate was so startling. I am also to respectfully suggest to you the appointment of a Ladies Committee, the members of which might be satisfactorily selected from residents in South

Africa, to be entrusted with a mission for the benefit of the natives, similar to that which has been so useful in the case of the Boer women and children.

I have the honour to be, Sir, your obedient servant

H R Fox Bourne

24 March 1902

Mr Chamberlain's reply, dated May 2, contained the following passages, and enclosed the report of the Superintendent of the Department:

I enclose a copy of the latest report on the working of the native camps in the Orange River Colony which has been received in this Department. It has since been ascertained by telegraph that in the native camps in the Transvaal, with a population of 40,000, the deaths in January were about 880, in February 550, and in March 400.

In the Orange River Colony, with a population of about 45,000 in native locations, the deaths were in January about 1400 in February 550, and in March about 470.

The figures given above appear to show that the conditions of life in the native camps have improved considerably, and Mr Chamberlain has no doubt that Lord Milner will not fail to exercise all proper care in dealing with the natives who are dependent on the Government.

I am, Sir, your obedient servant, Fred Graham,

To The Secretary to the Aborigines Protection Society, Native Refugee Department Bloemfontein, 2nd January 1902

Further enclosure from Chamberlain.

Sir, – I have the honour to forward herewith a copy of the November return for the native refugee camps in the Orange River Colony.

The several reports by the camp superintendent have been of a very satisfactory nature.

Discipline in the camps has been uniformly good, and the natives seem generally contented, and are readily turning out for work both with the Government and on the lands round the camps, which are being cultivated for their own benefit.

The death rate appears high, but, under the circumstances, I think it can be scarcely called excessive. Food has been scarce, and in many cases the natives had to put up with considerable privations before they were brought into the camps, and in addition, must be taken into consideration the invariable increase in the death-rate in this country due to the hot weather before the breaking of the rains, especially so in the case of young children.

Every effort is being made to deal with this matter.

Large supplies of comforts, such as milk, sugar, medicine, etc, are being distributed, and I am glad to say that at present there is every sign of a steady decrease of the sick list.

To sum up, l consider the report to show a very satisfactory state of affairs generally. The Department is now organised on a sound footing, and the natives themselves appear to thoroughly understand the present conditions of things, and to appreciate the efforts that are being made by His Majesty's Government on their behalf. I have, etc.

F Wilson Fox, Capt. Supt.

Native Refugee Department, ORC

On Emily's initial visit to Bloemfontein, she mentioned a population of approximately 1,500 in a native camp.

She also expressed, on several occasions, her desire to have someone sent out by the Society Of Friends, or the Aborigines' Protection Society, to assess the suffering that was rumoured to have been going on in the camps.

The restriction of movement imposed upon Emily meant she could do very little in response to accounts of maltreatment of the native population.

An example of the cursory information supplied by official sources can be seen in a detailed list of camp casualties published in The Times of July 25 1901.

The report ran to eight columns of references to white men, women and children in the camps in Natal, Cape Colony, Orange River Colony and the Transvaal.

Yet in a comparatively brief reference to the natives it was claimed that, of approximately 23,500 black people in the camps, only five deaths were reported – obviously a gross misrepresentation.

It was a sad reflection on those Victorian and Edwardian times that native people were treated as statistical components, slaves, and sometimes almost like cattle.

The treatment of black inmates in the mainly unlisted camps – the neglect, disease, starvation and death – are beyond description. The other white European nations were severely critical of the plight of the mainly Boer women and children, but when it came to the native internees, no voice of protest was heard.

PEACE IN SOUTH AFRICA

———❖———

EMILY was at last persuaded by friends and family to travel to the tranquil and picturesque shores of Lake Annecy, in France. She was still in a very delicate state of health, and it was felt that sun and silence would contribute to her recovery.

Emily was to stay for two months as a lone guest at an old converted Abbey. Her luggage contained papers, documents, editorials and correspondence relating to her recent privations.

Once she had sorted out the mass of manuscripts, Emily published a book, The Brunt Of The War And Where It Fell, which was her response to her critics.

On her way to Lake Annecy, Emily stayed overnight in Brussels where she met Annie Botha, the wife of General Louis Botha.

She had acted previously as a go-between for her husband and General Kitchener, resulting in a conference held in Middleburg on February 28 1901.

It took place on the very day when, having been boxed in by the British forces, Boer Generals DeWet and Steyn had crossed the Orange River, thus assuring their freedom to carry on the war. It was a serious obstacle to any peaceful settlement, which in the event, had eluded the Generals at the meeting.

Emily became quite friendly with the rather sophisticated Annie Botha, and after the war ended, was able to stay with the couple.

On April 12 1902, a delegation from the Boer side visited General Kitchener in Pretoria in an attempt to bargain for a peaceful solution to the war.

A second meeting took place on the morning of April 14. This first phase of a peace settlement ended on April 18 when the Boer delegation left Pretoria for further discussion among themselves.

After almost seven weeks, an agreement that the Anglo Boer war should be terminated was accepted by the British and Boer governments.

It was signed on May 31 1902, at five minutes past eleven in Vereeniging, just under an hour before deadline.

After everyone had signed, and upon shaking hands with the Boer representatives of the late Republics, Lord Kitchener remarked: "We are good friends now."

A few days later, on a lovely June morning, Emily was working quietly at her documentation when she looked at a newspaper and read about the peace treaty.

She was mindful of the problems that the women and children in the camps would face in their resettlement, many being widows with children, with no farms to return to.

President Steyn, who was not a well man, resigned on learning that his country would lose its independence.

Queen Victoria had died on January 22 1901 and her son Edward, had become King.

One of the basic terms of the peace pact was that, in laying down their arms, the Burghers were to acknowledge the King as sovereign.

This was a bone of contention in the eyes of many of the independently-minded Boers.

The bitter pill was sweetened somewhat with the agreement that civil government was to follow at the earliest opportunity.

One part of the agreement, later to erupt into major difficulties for many years, was the question of the native franchise which was not to be decided until a representative constitution had been granted.

Emily returned to England in time for the Coronation of King Edward VII on June 26 1902.

The Brunt Of The War And Where It Fell was published in 1902 but, despite having received some good appraisals, the public preferred to forget about the whole military debacle and the book did not enjoy a mass sale.

The final text of the peace treaty included reparations by the British Government to the Boers of £3,000,000.

The money was partially for the resettlement of prisoners and internees, and assistance toward the reinstatement of the farms and the whole fabric of the rural society which had been a casualty of the scorched earth campaign of Lords Roberts and Kitchener and their army commanders.

Sir Alfred Milner had been installed as Governor of the Orange River Colony and the Transvaal, which was then administered on a constitution typical of the Crown Colony system.

In order to underwrite it, a large loan was granted by the Home Government to be repaid through taxation of the gold production in the Transvaal.

A Royal Commission report to the new King, presented by Viscount Esher, chairman of the War Office Reconstitution Committee, was not good for Lord Roberts, who had placed the blame for farm burning mainly on his young colonels.

The report also stated that if the pre-war objections of the Liberals had been heeded, the expenditure of approximately £200,000,000 could have been avoided, and hundreds of lives would not have been forfeited.

In the first stages of the peace settlement, Lord Milner had instituted a Land Board, whose brief was to aid many of the impatient Boer combatants by the acquisition of land for them.

Lord Milner's energetic private secretary, John Buchan (the author and future Governor General of Canada) helped to galvanise the Board into action, although the aid was insufficient for the needs of the displaced Boer women and children.

Emily, now that martial law had been lifted, and with new funds available, decided to return to South Africa to try to help the war casualties.

In August 1902, the defeated Boer Generals Botha, De La Rey, and De Wet, visited London in an attempt to raise more money for their suffering people.

They were welcomed by King Edward VII, and Joseph Chamberlain took on responsibility for the relief of the orphans and the destitute. He also promised suitable Government help for the widows.

The three Boer Generals then proceeded to Europe for more fundraising. The president of the Carnegie Steel Corporation of America gave $100,000 to Louis Botha for the use of orphans and widows of the war.

Emily returned to South Africa on May 12 1903 on the RMS Carisbrook Castle. Having had briefings in Cape Town, and on obtaining visiting permits, Emily visited Beaufort West, where she met and made friends with Olive Schreiner, an author and civil rights activist.

Emily then travelled to Springfontein and Bloemfontein where she met a judge, Barry Hertzog, who told her that the £3,000,000 of British Government Relief Funds was being distributed badly.

Emily had been invited to meet various gatherings of Boer people but she did not wish to be seen as a political creature.

In her dealings with the authorities she was logical, businesslike and often very cool over delays and administrative complications. But she could be abrupt and to the point at times, much to the chagrin of officials, though she was never rude or emotional.

Once again, taken to the hearts of the mainly Boer population, Emily began to be named The Angel Of Love.

She continued her task of distributing clothing and food to those in need, and also involved herself in agricultural problems. The need to replant crops had become of real concern as food was already running short.

On behalf of her Relief Committee, Emily began a policy of helping the more destitute farmers by distributing grain, seed and bags of ready-to-use meal.

She even bought and supplied teams of oxen to be given to the farmers and passed from farmstead to farmstead.

Emily was becoming a symbol of hope to the needy and many homes and buildings displayed photographs of the woman they called The Angel Of Love.

Emily was beginning to suffer from tiredness as well as neuritis in some of her joints which she put down to constant travel along rugged roads and tracks.

Her heart was also showing early signs of being over-stressed. Breathing, when walking and climbing even gentle slopes, especially in high country, became difficult.

Just prior to Christmas 1903, after yet another strenuous mercy mission, Emily returned to London.

She had been prompted to help the Boer farmers as a result of the failure of the harvest, due to a drought in 1903. Coinciding with this, there had been a serious economic depression causing the industrial situation to become even more dire than the agricultural scene.

The lack of native miners threatened the economic development of South Africa, and the economy was also held back by the need to spend heavily on repairing the massive war damage.

When peace came, administrators and miners enthusias-tically flocked back to the mines, but the essential part of the operation – the native workers – were not available.

Labour was being absorbed elsewhere, and there could be

no rapid expansion. By April 1903, the Chamber of Mines decided to solve the problem by introducing Chinese labour and the Legislative Council was asked to approve it.

Initially, in the UK, the importation of Asiatics was strongly deprecated by many. So upon Emily's arrival in the UK, Chinese labour for the Rand mines was of national interest.

Sir Alfred Lyttelton told the House of Commons: "It is the desire of the Transvaal people to have Asiatic labour for the mines."

That was not really the case, as the decision had been made by the Legislative Council. But after a three-day debate, the motion was carried by 22 to four, the majority including nine unofficial members.

The Boer leaders were alarmed at Sir Alfred's statement and a petition signed by them against the mass importation was sent to the Colonial Office.

Emily, who knew the Boer leaders, became involved in the Chinese labour issue. She discussed it with prominent Liberal MPs, wrote a letter to The Manchester Guardian, addressed a public meeting at Caxton Hall in London, and generally became politically as well as socially involved.

The Times was in favour of the importation of Chinese labour, and it does appear that Emily was getting out of her depth in her sympathies with the Boer leaders.

One backlash centred on a private letter the Boer General Smuts had written to Emily, which she thought should be in the public domain and sent to The Times.

Written in February 1903, it condemned the intention to import Chinese labour in the strongest of terms.

General Smuts castigated Lord Milner and the mining industry, saying that eighty per cent of them were bogus concerns.

"We were merrily spinning to perdition," he wrote in despair.

Despite Emily's good intentions, publication of the letter sparked an immediate outcry against General Smuts. The reaction almost cost the General his appointment as a recently-installed Minister of the Crown.

Emily profusely apologised to the General, and always regretted publishing his letter.

The General bore Emily no ill will, despite what he described as a storm of execration in Johannesburg, especially from the mining organisations.

When the Liberals were returned to Government in 1905, they commenced to curb Chinese indentured labour, and Emily was acknowledged as having precipitated the policy.

During 1904, Emily remained concerned for the young Boer women who were living in poverty, many of them on isolated farmsteads. She developed an interest in home industry occupations, such as tapestry and lace making.

Local government had already embarked on a policy of education for the younger element of the Boer society. But Emily felt that the older females were in need, too.

The committee had agreed in November of that year that the time had arrived for the winding-up of the South

African Women And Children's Distress Fund. It also agreed that a new organisation with the same committee should be instituted and called the Boer Home Industries Aid Society.

Emily, in response to the needs of the Boer women, began to learn lace making, spinning and weaving.

She made a new friend, Alice Green, and they went to Ireland where they studied the home industries.

She also studied the making of blankets, rugs, tweeds and suit and dress material. She also took a great interest in the construction of spinning wheels and looms.

After meeting Margaret Clark, a young well-educated Quaker, they both decided to visit South Africa.

In response to an offer of suitable premises in Philippolis, Orange River Colony, the two women arrived in South Africa in February 1905.

The premises in Philippolis were provided by the Rev Colin Fraser, the father of Isabel Steyn, and on March 13 1905, the Weaving And Craft School began with a nucleus of six young women pupils, soon rising to 13.

The basic idea of the cottage industry was to encourage pupils to pass on their newly-acquired skills to other young women. Thus an ever-expanding source of self-help began to materialise.

As the school became established, the rugs, mats, general dress and suit material, and even the cotton dish and floor cloths were greatly admired.

However, Philippolis, being rather isolated and with limited water facilities, was no longer an ideal place in which to expand. Emily was offered alternative accommodation by Dr Kriel at a Johannesburg orphanage in Langlaagte.

She agreed to teach some of the inmates over 12 years of age in a special shed.

Generous help, both financial and material, was also arriving from France and Switzerland.

The initial industry at Philippolis remained with Margaret Clark as superintendent, while at the Langlaagte orphanage, production and teaching was also maturing into an amazing success with Constance Cloete acting as Emily's companion teacher.

Emily found herself surrounded by masses of admiring orphans whenever she went out for a quiet stroll.

After a stay of 10 months, toward the end of 1905, Margaret Clark returned home.

She was sorely missed by Emily, who appreciated her as a tremendously dedicated teacher and worker.

Margaret's vacancy was quickly filled by Marion Rowntree, another dedicated teacher.

Now that both establishments were on a sound, self-sufficient footing, Emily decided she should slowly withdraw from regular school engagements.

In February 1907, whilst she was a guest of the Steyns, she had begun to feel unwell. Bellevue, where she was staying, was at quite a high altitude and the rarified air was an additional hazard to her.

She had been aware of her heart condition, became easily exhausted, was a victim of repetitive nosebleeds, and suffered from vertigo.

Emily's weaving and cloth production schools were proving a self-sufficient success and her endeavours were also recognised by the Boer leaders, such as General Smuts, Botha and other influential men.

Emily's reputation as The Angel Of Love had been truly and permanently established in South Africa.

DEAR MR GANDHI...

ON HER return to England, in view of her delicate state of health, Emily began wondering whether to settle in a warmer Mediterranean climate. But despite her illness, she maintained her involvement in women's rights.

In the closing months of 1908, she had attended two important public meetings in support of Women's Suffrage.

The first was at the Queen's Hall in London, and the second on the following day at the Albert Hall where she was once again on the public stage with David Lloyd George.

Emily went to Italy early in 1909 and while in Rome, she suffered from angina. It emerged that she had an enlarged heart, which almost proved to be fatal.

Emily continued to keep in touch with General Smuts through long letters to which he always responded in similar vein.

In the meantime, her health gradually improved, though she was no longer very physically active.

Emily had been approached by influential Free State representatives of the South African Federation in September 1912 to unveil a national monument in Bloemfontein.

The ceremony was to be in December 1913 and Emily decided to go for it. But by the time she arrived in South Africa again on September 13 1913, her health had deteriorated due to her progressive heart condition and her journey to Bloemfontein had to be abandoned.

She returned to the Cape Town area where the atmosphere at sea level made it easier to breathe and was thus less demanding on her heart.

At the unveiling ceremony at the national memorial in Bloemfontein, Charles Fichardt read a speech in Afrikaans and English that Emily had written.

There were many thousands in attendance on that day to hear her speech imploring the people to forgive their enemies, and to avoid hatred of others, which she stated was like a rust corroding away the soul of individuals and nations.

She also commented that "noble character", as opposed to material prosperity by Statesmen, formed the basis of a great nation.

In referring to Dingaan's Day, the memorial day of the Boers' victory over the Zulus, Emily berated nations for continuing to spend great sums of money on killing each other in their lust for land and gold.

In appealing to the women, she asked them to be merciful to the weak and downtrodden, and to be aware of the foes of freedom, namely selfishness and tyranny.

Copies of Emily's speech were printed in leaflet form and widely distributed.

One person who might have been impressed by her speech was the Indian leader, Mahatma Gandhi.

A long-term resident in South Africa, Gandhi had become a civil rights campaigner on behalf of his fellow

Indians. There were many discriminatory laws in existence against the Indian population, and among the most provocative measures, which applied to all non-white people, were the pass laws.

On a previous occasion, Gandhi had been arrested for not having a pass, which a non-white individual was compelled to carry at night.

Another racial factor was the Natal government's intention to disenfranchise all Indian residents – a measure to ensure Natal should remain white-dominated.

The white racists feared the country would soon be swamped by Indian immigrants.

Gandhi had drawn up a petition against the measures and organised the Natal Indian Congress Party. In 1906 he appeared in England, where he pleaded the cause of the South African Indians.

He was advised to wait until a new Government was installed in the Transvaal.

There was further opposition to the discriminatory laws in South Africa.

When joined by a large representation of Chinese, under the leadership of Leong Quinn, the Indians, under Gandhi, organised a passive resistance campaign in July 1907.

Gandhi challenged Transvaal Law when the Immigration Act decreed that all immigrants had to register their fingerprints to prevent forging of documents.

Gandhi flatly refused to comply, and in marching at the head of a crowd of protesters, he was arrested and jailed for a year.

Some years later, Gandhi demonstrated again just after the union of the four provinces of South Africa.

In an attempt to force the Government to repeal the immigration tax, Gandhi marched at the head of 3,000 Indians from Natal province, over the Transvaal border.

On entry, he was escorted to the jail in Bloemfontein, under arrest once again.

He had embarked on a permanent campaign of Satyagraha (civil disobedience of discriminatory laws). He was not a person the Boer leaders could negotiate with, nor did they like him.

Gandhi sought Emily's help as he felt she was the ideal person to intercede for recognition of the status of the educated Indian and the various Boer leaders had previously refused to meet him for any reason.

Despite their ethnic differences, Emily shared many of Mahatma Gandhi's characteristics.

They both campaigned in a tenacious, non-violent fashion in the face of governmental and public opposition.

Their moral courage in the support of human rights was second to none.

But the difference between them became evident later when Gandhi was revered in almost God-like terms by the mass of his own people.

But Emily, during her later years and after her death, was conveniently forgotten by many of her compatriots, which is a sad reflection on the so-called magnanimous attitude of British society.

At the time of Gandhi's approach to her, Emily had been

convalescing at the Cape Town residence of General Botha where her friends included former President Steyn.

Additionally, she had been maintaining frequent and friendly correspondence with General Smuts since the end of the Boer hostilities.

No doubt Gandhi was aware of Emily's close friendship with these immensely powerful statesmen.

General Smuts in particular would not even entertain speaking to, let alone negotiating with the Mahatma, hence the reason for his approach to her.

Gandhi, who had frequently clashed with General Smuts over quite some time, bore no grudge against him.

Indeed, while in jail at one time in Pretoria, Gandhi made the General a stout pair of leather sandals as a gesture of respect and friendship which matured in subsequent years, especially when the Mahatma left South Africa finally to return to India.

WORLD WAR ONE

———⊶◦⊷———

FROM the moment World War One erupted, Emily was opposed to it, as indeed were many other Europeans. Emily had taken up residence in Bude, Cornwall, when once again she became involved in anti-war activities.

At the commencement of the war, a conciliation document called An International Manifesto Of Women had been been drawn up and issued by the International Women's Suffrage Alliance.

Copies had been delivered to all foreign embassies, including the British Office in London.

Moving once again despite her delicate condition, first to Italy then Holland, Emily was temporarily appointed Secretary for the Women's International Bureau in May 1915.

Her primary aim was for peace, tolerance and understanding throughout the world.

In the meantime, the belligerent countries were determined to continue the conflict, each side being under the impression that ultimate victory was within their grasp.

International peace and conciliation, promoted mainly by women, remained only a dream.

On May 1 1916, a demonstration took place in Berlin. It was led by Karl Liebknecht, in a public place, and took a great deal of courage to enact. Liebknecht and his few supporters declared their opposition to the hostilities by shouting out from a public area "Down with the war" and "Down with the Government".

After his arrest, Liebknecht was sentenced to four years' imprisonment by a military court.

As a mark of solidarity, 50,000 munitions workers downed tools in support.

Other protests broke out in various German towns, which highlighted the German minority's anti-war position. This in turn was a reflection of a growing international socialist opposition to hostilities as casualties grew.

Emily was still determined that the bloodshed should be brought to an end.

While in Switzerland, she planned to visit German-occupied Belgium, and indeed the belligerent Germany, to talk with women having similar peace-loving aims.

On May 3 1916, Emily's presence at a pacifist meeting was noticed by the British authorities.

Emily also wished to see, if possible, the internees at Ruhleben, a German camp for British civilians near Berlin.

In the process she met Baron von Romberg, the German Minister, who provided passes for her to enter Belgium and Germany.

Despite her generally weak condition, Emily was prepared to embark on the visit but was apprehensive about her possible reception in Germany.

She was also aware of the moral indignation that would be generated back in the United Kingdom.

Despite her reservations, she finally left Switzerland for Belgium and Germany. One of the conditions for her entry, especially into Belgium, was that she should sleep every night during her visit in the Belgian capital, Brussels.

It was not considered prudent for Emily to interview Belgian nationals, and she was to be continually accompanied by a Baron Falkenhausen, her guide and escort.

Falkenhausen had once been a student at King's College, Cambridge, and had a wife in Berlin.

In visiting places such as communal kitchens, Emily soon discovered that there was a lot of tuberculosis among the Belgians, thought to have been caused by malnutrition and deficiency of diet.

That was a direct result of the blockade of imports against Germany, her allies, and occupied countries.

Once again, as the result of war, the innocent were suffering extreme hardship.

On June 17, Emily was informed that she had been granted permission to visit the German capital, Berlin. Accompanied by Baron Falkenhausen, she left the same day.

On arrival, the Baron was met by his wife, and Emily was installed at a hotel where she had a room complete with a telephone. One of her first actions was to write to the German Foreign Minister, thanking him for his endeavours to facilitate her visit.

In the meantime, Emily had been contacted by the German equivalent of the Peace Committee, and had also paid a visit to Dr Alice Salamon, an internationally-known

169

nutritionist. It appeared that although bread, potatoes and vegetables were reasonably obtainable, there was a dire shortage of meat, causing tremendous queues outside butchers' shops. Otherwise the diet, although bland, was reasonable.

In response to her letter to the Foreign Minister, Emily was granted an interview during which the Minister said he was pleased with Emily's contact with the nutritionist.

The Minister also announced that she could see and interview whoever she wished while in Germany.

This was much to the relief of her escort, Baron Falkenhausen, who until that interview had a much tighter custodial brief.

During the visit, it appeared that there were a number of German militarists who, together with the many Social Democrats, would never be disposed to a humiliating surrender.

In visiting the civilian internment camp in Ruhleben, Emily witnessed the monotony and strain of the British internees.

She found that problems were entirely different to those she discovered on her visits to the South African camps 16 years previously.

Although devoid of work or amusement, there was no indication of disease, starvation and death.

Food was adequate, but mental strain, complemented by anxiety about future events, was evident mainly among the older men.

Emily discussed the problems with the senior British

Captain at the camp, promising on her return to England to strive for the release of at least some of the other inmates.

To Emily's relief, she found no evidence of maladministration or starvation at the camp.

It should be borne in mind that the visit by Emily to Belgium and Germany could have turned out very differently.

In the preceding September of 1915, a woman of a similar disposition and background to Emily had been executed by a German firing squad.

Like Emily, she had been the daughter of a clergyman, and had become the first Matron of the Belgian School Of Nursing at the Berkendael Institute in Brussels.

She had been arrested by the German military authorities for helping Allied soldiers escape from enemy-occupied territory, was subsequently tried by a German military court, and summarily executed.

This humane woman, so dedicated to the sick and suffering, became, through her untimely death, a martyr.

Her name has been constantly revered and remembered. It was Nurse Edith Cavell.

After leaving Germany and again entering Switzerland en route for the United Kingdom through France, Emily went to the British Legation where she was informed that she would probably not be welcome while travelling through France.

At the French border, she was strip-searched, her passport was minutely scrutinised, and it became evident that her name had been well documented in an index system which referred to her history and character as a pacifist.

Eventually, she was passed over to an English official and her return to Southampton had also been noted by the British authorities.

Later in 1916, when news of Emily's visit to enemy territory became public, the purpose of her journey became misrepresented. Questions were being asked in Parliament, which was an embarrassment to many MPs and officials.

In November, it was even suggested by one MP that through undertaking such a visit to Germany, and German-occupied territory, Emily might have been guilty of a punishable offence.

In answering this and other relevant questions, Sir Frederick Smith, the Attorney General, voicing official legal opinion, stated that she had committed no criminal offence because she had gained contact with the enemy from neutral territory.

By entering and leaving Germany through neutral Switzerland, it was not an indictable offence in the eyes of British law.

Emily found herself in the national news once again, especially in such papers as The Times, in which the letters appeared to be anti-Hobhouse on most occasions.

The main springboard of the attack upon her humanitarian endeavours was that Emily had decided to visit enemy-occupied territory prior to her being in Switzerland.

Emily was once again drawn into the public arena and forced to defend herself. This she did by virtue of a letter to The Times, which was dated November 8 1916 and published the following week. Emily's letter, while rubbishing erroneous statements in Parliament and the Press regarding her movements, categorically denied that she had conceived any idea of visiting Germany prior to being in the neutral territory of Switzerland.

She also stated that she went to Germany openly, under her own name, with a humanitarian pass.

In concluding that she had travelled in the interests of humanity, peace and truth, she added that she was proud and thankful that she had embarked on such a mission.

The wolves of criticism and derision had been answered by Emily's personal testimony.

Her peaceful humanitarian visit to enemy territory, having become the subject of national interest, had revealed a flaw in Government regulations.

It generated a proposal to invoke a new regulation, under the Defence Of The Realm Act, making a visit to enemy territory by a British National an offence under any circumstances.

1916 proved to be yet another very eventful year in the Great War's progress. Women, who had volunteered to help the war effort by replacing male employees who were being enlisted in vast numbers into the armed forces, were proving themselves very efficient and successful in taking over the jobs of their male counterparts.

In February 1916, food shortages in Germany sparked off riots in Berlin and the British Government announced an intention to create a Ministry Of Blockade, thus worsening the German food and war materials shortage.

Meanwhile, male workers found it hard to accept that women could work as well as men.

One example of this happened on March 18, when women dockers in Liverpool were forced to withdraw their labour because the male dockers refused to work with them.

During 1916, the Boer Generals Jan Smuts and Louis Botha found themselves back in the headlines.

Smuts in particular, once a powerful Boer adversary and during the Great War a staunch British friend and ally, had successfully campaigned against the Germans in East Africa.

On June 7, the Secretary for War, Lord Kitchener, was reported as having drowned when HMS Hampshire was mined and sunk to the west of the Orkneys.

He had been on passage with his staff as principal officer in a delegation to Russia. It was stated that he had remained to the end a true hero to the people.

As a final devastating farewell to the months of summer, British casualty figures for August alone had risen to 127,000.

The number of British casualties rose dramatically when on October 31 1916, British casualty figures in excess of 350,000 were announced for the preceding three-month period.

The number of women being involved in the war effort had also dramatically increased. On November 14 1916, it was officially reported that 3.2 million women were thus engaged.

A further reference to the military casualty list gave sombre evidence of the gravity of the situation. On November 28, a French Government report listing the number of dead at the battle of the Somme quoted the Allies at 500,000, and the Germans at 650,000.

In December 1916, David Lloyd George had become the new Prime Minister.

He had previously been made Secretary for War in place of the deceased Lord Kitchener and had said the UK's war aim was Germany's complete downfall.

But the year ended with a stalemate in the trenches on the Western Front.

There was a terrible foreboding that there was worse to come, when during Christmas, figures were quoted of losses of 700,000 men at Verdun while, at the battle of Somme, a further 650,000 Allied soldiers had perished. Most of the victims of the mass slaughter were British.

One glimmer of hope during the terrible year did appear on Emily's horizon, due to her visit to the camp in Ruhleben.

During August, she had been informed by Lord Newton at the Foreign Office that negotiations with the German Government were proceeding for the exchange of civilian internees. This was in response to Emily's promise to intercede with a suggestion that all internees over the age of 45 years should be repatriated. In addition, she proposed that all those of military age should be placed in a neutral country.

In early 1917, General Smuts came to Britain and was

appointed a member of the British War Cabinet. The British Prime Minister had decided that "England could not, under any circumstances, afford to lose the services of the man".

But Emily, through her friendship and correspondence, and with her non-belligerent actions, was at times an embarrassment to the great soldier.

On April 6 1917, America hastened the end by declaring war on Germany and standing alongside Britain and France and their allies.

By the time the armistice had been declared in 1918, 10 million people had perished, of which 750,000 were British and 200,000 were from the British Empire – a third of them Indian soldiers.

In the light of this, Emily's efforts to avoid war, although futile, were nonetheless a magnificent humanitarian gesture.

The Aftermath Of War

A T THE END of the Great War, Emily was approaching retirement age. There was a shortage of food in Britain, though no starvation, due in the main to the German U-Boat blockade.

Conversely, on the Continent, especially in Germany, many children were suffering from the ravages of under-nourishment, and reduced in many cases to starvation level.

Emily threw her unbounding energy and dedication into doing something about it.

One priority was to raise money for the Swiss Relief Fund For Starving Children. Emily set about raising money for the fund which aimed to transport starving children from Austria, Czechoslovakia, Hungary and Germany to recover in private houses and nursing homes in Switzerland.

Emily also embarked on a fund for the Russian children who were starving – The Russian Babies Fund.

Emily was chairman, with the usual brief of supplying sustenance, mainly milk products, plus baby clothing, through the Russian supply system based in Petrograd.

Leonard, Emily's brother, was also instrumental in raising funds for the initiative, which inaugurated in July 1919.

Emily was also a member of the Fight The Famine Council which campaigned for justice for people in Europe who were suffering from the effects of the post-war blockade.

From that grew the internationally-renowned organisation Save The Children. It offered relief and succour to innocent victims of war, flood, drought, disease and famine. It was one of the greatest humanitarian commitments and undertakings for the benefit of the children of the world.

Founded by Eglantyne Jebb and her sister Dorothy Buxton, the first two honorary secretaries, its desire to deliver practical relief to the suffering was shared by Emily Hobhouse.

Many of the early workers, a large number of them women, experienced dangerous conditions, especially in the ravaged war zones in which their humanitarian relief work was carried out.

In its early days, Save The Children made grants available to such organisations as Emily's.

Eglantyne Jebb also set up the Save The Children International Union in Geneva, an alliance of other benevolent organisations in other countries with the aim of speeding up and quickly applying relief wherever it was needed.

The success of this today is a great tribute to this remarkable woman.

Like her, Emily was one of many unsung heroines who were working in Europe at the time.

Rations in Vienna provided 900 calories per day. This was supplemented by an American relief organisation, providing extra food.

In Leipzig, where there was no extra relief, rations were slightly better at 1,200 calories per day.

Prior to the issue of the report, Emily had already (despite her poor state of health), offered assistance and worked among the children of Leipzig.

There was an offer of aid from a Baron Schroeder, enabling Emily to proceed with a programme of extra nourishment for a large number of the children. She also received aid from Prince Max of Baden and the Grand Duchess.

Emily also inspired many other German individuals and organisations to assist. The Deutsche Bank co-ordinated further aid and yet more help came from a group of American Quakers.

Save The Children, with Swiss and United Kingdom organisations, also continued to provide very generous financial help.

The main purpose of the plan was to supplement the children's diet by a daily provision of extra food at their schools. This, to many of the children, was their only substantial daily meal, and 1,000 children benefited every day in the Leipzig schools.

In order to avoid depletion of local food stocks, the provisions were mainly purchased in the formerly neutral countries of Denmark and Sweden. The shopping list included flour, rice, potatoes, beans, cheese, chocolate, dried fruit, cooking oils, pasta, peas, sausages, semolina, and sugar. The Danish Red Cross organisation also gave valuable support.

In expanding her horizons, Emily appealed for goodwill from South Africa, which elicited a very generous response.

General Smuts was Prime Minister at the time of her request for help and his Government reacted positively.

Emily's old friend, Isabel Steyn, also contributed enthusiastically to the funding of the Leipzig scheme.

All this help enabled aid to continue well into mid-summer 1922.

However, Emily was forced through ill health to leave Leipzig in the latter part of 1920. After physically collapsing, she was admitted to hospital, due to her heart condition.

During her recuperation, Emily returned to Bude in Cornwall, where she was advised to take a complete rest for at least a month.

By mid November, Emily had returned to Leipzig, albeit in a delicate state of health, and embarked once again on her good Samaritan work.

As part of her recuperation she was on her way to Lucerne, where she stayed until April 1921.

During the previous winter, one of her legs had become paralysed. She returned straight to London, where she stayed with her brother Leonard in Wimbledon.

Physical Deterioration

I N EARLY 1921, due to the kind initiative of Isabel Steyn, Emily's South African friends and admirers had collected the purchase price of a house for her. Having been reduced to living in quite a frugal manner, Emily was overwhelmed with gratitude at the generous and spontaneous gesture.

On receiving the money, she was able to acquire a house in the beautiful resort of St Ives, West Cornwall, the haven of many famous artists.

She was very happy, and felt really secure and comfortable at home, having settled in by Christmas 1921.

Emily's social contribution, and her undaunted efforts in the face of great opposition and difficulties, was duly appreciated by the Leipzig authorities.

A marble bust of Emily was given pride of place, and permanently displayed, in the Rathaus in Leipzig.

She was also presented with a tablet and document of appreciation for her dedicated work.

In 1925, Emily was also the recipient of a decoration presented by the German Red Cross Society.

Due to her discipline and drive, and in spite of illness and extreme difficulties, Emily prevailed against all opposition and stood out as a bewildering female factor in a mainly male-dominated society.

Despite her almost superhuman attributes, the fact that she was encased in a now frail human body finally became evident.

During the winter of 1922, Emily's health began to deteriorate rapidly to the point that she was unable to negotiate the stairs in her house in St Ives.

She was forced to sleep on a chairbed in a downstairs room that had been used as a study.

With angina and asthma, she was often forced to rest in bed and could not even walk to her own front gate.

With no possibility of obtaining the services of a care worker, by July 1923 she sold her house in St Ives and went to London where she temporarily acquired a small flat.

She remained deeply interested in social affairs, having written, and had published in South Africa, a book entitled War Without Glamour. It depicted war at its ugliest, and told of the innocent sufferers of conflict. As an historical document, it was a very appealing literary contribution to the need for lasting peace throughout the world.

Emily also maintained a keen interest in South African affairs. In 1924, Dr Hertzog's National Party, in an alliance with the Labour Party, defeated General Smuts, whom Emily considered was presenting an imperialistic profile.

She was supportive of the victors, but did however, show great unease over Hertzog's lock-out policy in the segregation of coloured South Africans. Segregation of people, she felt, by way of colour, race, or creed, was against the principles of human rights and democratic freedom.

In 1925, Emily moved to the Chichester area, where she

rented a small bungalow near the sea. It proved to be eminently unsuitable for someone as disabled as she was. The bungalow had inadequate insulation and was draughty in the cold windy weather.

Being away from close contact with her many friends, and with only an inexperienced young girl to look after her, she began to feel apprehensive about her future.

Emily needed a friendlier and warmer environment and moved to the Isle of Wight. In January 1926, she suffered from a serious bout of pleurisy. She was visited by her brother and sister, Leonard and Maud.

Although at the time she was seriously ill, it was not expected to be terminal. But by the first day of June, her condition had become critical.

She was transferred by ambulance from the Isle of Wight to a London nursing home, where she died on June 8 1926.

Although she died peacefully, Emily had suffered a great deal of pain, coughing continually from the effects of her pleurisy, which had put a tremendous strain on her already weakened heart.

It was found later that the pleurisy was the result of a tumour that had been well established deep inside Emily's chest.

After her death, a service was held at St Mary's Church in Kensington for members of her family, friends and admirers.

One of Emily's final wishes, which was duly respected, was for her ashes to be interred in South Africa.

This personal request was honoured, probably in a way

that she would never have expected. The ashes were interred during a service of honour at the base of the Women's Memorial in Bloemfontein – a sacred place in South African eyes.

Until then, only President Steyn and General de Wet had been interred at the memorial.

Such was the feeling in South Africa over the loss of the great woman that when the interment of her ashes was conducted on 27 October 1926, all national and municipal flags in the area were flown at half mast while shops and business premises were also closed in Bloemfontein.

For miles around, people descended in vast numbers to mourn the passing of The Angel Of Love.

Emily's remains, in a casket, were placed on a bier, suitably draped, in a church bedecked with masses of flowers and wreaths.

The funeral procession from the church to the final resting place at the memorial was very moving.

The casket containing her ashes was solemnly taken to its ultimate resting place by six girls.

Two of them were girls from the weaving schools that Emily had founded; two were the granddaughters of Presidents Kruger and Steyn, and the remaining two girls were actually named Emily Hobhouse.

Following the bearers were several hundred schoolgirls all wearing white head-dresses which were also veils.

There also a vast procession of students, many dressed in their black gowns and mortar boards.

The seemingly endless procession included a very large

group of mounted burghers. Many of the men had been former inmates in the concentration camps.

A very large column of individual mourners, and a large number of cars transporting VIPs, formed part of the vast procession.

In addition, there were crowds of indigenous people, Indians, and Chinese immigrants.

At the moment of final interment, a flock of white doves were released as a sign of peace and goodwill.

Also present were a large company of Boer Commandoes who discharged a volley from the rifles they were carrying in a final tribute to the memory of Emily.

The great statesman, Jan Smuts, delivered an eloquent and memorable speech in Emily's honour.

His concluding words referred to the once unknown woman from England who influenced permanently the course of the history of South Africa in becoming a great symbol of reconciliation.

Mahatma Gandhi referred to Emily as "one of the noblest and bravest of women".

He spoke of the soul of this frail woman, rising against the barbarity of the concentration camps, in the face of insults, imprisonment, and military obstruction, with the great courage of a true heroine.

He urged Indian women to follow Emily's example and remarked that she remained chaste, and that her life, being pure as crystal, was dedicated to God's service.

He also requested that the memory of this great woman should be treasured.

One of Emily's attributes, during her lifetime, was her struggle against predominantly violent attitudes.

Mahatma Gandhi, in referring to non-violence, depicted it as the greatest force at the disposal of mankind, being mightier than the mightiest weapon of destruction devised by the ingenuity of man.

The following poem, Now With This Love, by Mary Morison Webster, is commended as an appropriate tribute to this great Cornish woman, Emily Hobhouse.

Now with this love, I shall walk regally,
Henceforth I shall go proudly as a queen,
No longer sorrow-bowed for what hath been,
But joyful in the things that are to be,
Now all men shall see beauty grow in me,
And loveliness that springs from thoughts unseen,
Shall be expressed in word and mien;
I shall forgo my old humility.
Now doth my love endow me with new pride,
Now joy becomes me like a wedding-dress,
Now all my days are filled with graciousness,
And hope and peace walk ever by my side;
I go so crowned to all men, but to thee,
Yielding myself, I yield all sovereignty.

THE INFLUENCE OF THE TIMES

A PARTICULARLY disingenuous article reporting Emily's death under the headline "Humanitarian Zeal" was published in The Times. The article, referring initially to Emily's prominence in the South African and First World War, alleged a lack of sound knowledge and judgement due to her humanitarian zeal.

With reference to her work in reporting back on the concentration camps, The Times stated that conditions in the camps were largely unavoidable, with the mortality rate being partly the fault of the occupants.

The article, full of chicanery in its ill-founded portrayal, would have been described in modern jargon as "being economical with the truth".

It will be recalled that throughout her great humanitarian crusades, Emily Hobhouse had constantly been the target of criticism in various articles published in The Times.

It is also a fact that there were many gentlemen's and senior military officers' clubs, especially in the big cities, where no women would have been permitted to encroach on the privacy of the men.

The organisations, with their elite membership, were considered to be the epitome of the bulwark and influence of the British Empire.

One of the principal newspapers widely circulated

around these establishments, upholding Britain's imperial traditions in the male-dominated environment, was The Times.

The manager of the paper, himself a dedicated imperialist, was C F Moberly Bell. Sometimes, articles were printed to disparage Emily's reports, with the object of upholding the good name of the Empire and making her claims appear seriously exaggerated.

An example of this is a report written by Flora Shaw, a well-known author of the day.

She had written many articles, mainly on foreign affairs for The Times, and had been acclaimed as an acknowledged expert on colonial affairs.

In parallel with Emily Hobhouse, she deplored the outbreak of the South African War, but there, the comparison between the two women abruptly ended.

During the war, Flora Shaw, a dedicated imperialist, wrote a series of articles for The Times upholding the British case as clearly as possible.

The articles, at the request of the Foreign Office, were officially reprinted for circulation in America and translated so they could be read on the Continent. Such was the cosy relationship between the Government, Moberly Bell of The Times, and the influential Flora Shaw.

In early December 1901, Flora heard ugly stories being circulated about brutality and terrible conditions in the South African concentration camps.

As she did not believe the stories of injustice perpetrated by the Government, she embarked on a journey to the

Cape to see conditions for herself. When Moberly Bell heard of her intention, he begged her to go on behalf of The Times.

Her Camp visit report was undated but appears to have referred to late January to February 1902, a year after Emily's initial visit.

Her report is particularly interesting as it is in almost direct contradiction to that of Emily Hobhouse only 12 months earlier. It read:

Flora spent an interesting morning visiting one of the much abused concentration camps outside Bloemfontein.

Here were nearly 7,000 refugees, living in an admirably organised camp, laid out in broad streets and blocks of tents.

Flora examined everything with the greatest interest; she saw the children in the schools, the soup kitchen which fed 2,000 children twice a day, the arrangements for washing, for mending shoes and for providing all the necessities for civilised existence; she enquired into the "sorrowfully high" child mortality, and learned that it was due almost entirely to the heat, for there was no shade at all, not a tree in sight, and the bell tents were inevitably stifling.

In comparison with Emily's prior report, there is no reason to doubt that both ladies were relating an honest, unbiased account of their visit, albeit that Flora Shaw's visit was more of a brief morning tour.

The Ladies' Commission attendance, under the leadership of Millicent Fawcett, had published a report similar to the findings of the Hobhouse account, about a year prior to Flora Shaw's report.

It can only be concluded that if Flora Shaw's optimistic report on the camp is credible, then Emily Hobhouse must have achieved outstanding success in bringing about improvements for the internees.

Later, Flora Shaw married Sir Frederick Lugard, thus acquiring the title of Lady Lugard, and was made a Dame in honour of her authorship and services to the Crown.

Epilogue

—————⎯⟫⬦⟪⎯—————

EMILY Hobhouse has been revered for her humanitarian deeds in many other countries. In France, for example, Edmund Rostand, the poet and author of Cyrano De Bergerac, was an avid admirer of Emily's work and wrote a long poem in her honour.

Published in December 1901, it was entitled Ballade De Miss Hobhouse and translated into English, Dutch and Italian with a very wide circulation.

The actions of this outstanding woman have inspired many modern women to participate in national and international affairs.

She was a pioneering example of the Suffragette movement's slogan "deeds not words".

To further honour her memory, a South African postage stamp, bearing Emily's portrait, was issued on 8 June 1976, in commemoration of the 50th anniversary of her death.

The South African navy, in recognition of her fame, even had a submarine named Emily Hobhouse – not that she would have been happy in being associated with such an instrument of death and destruction.

A further South African honour to Emily can be found today in Cornwall, where the village of St Ive is divided by the modern A390 roadway passing through. This recently laid road has cannibalised part of St Ive churchyard. In Emily's day it would have been a much narrower roadway, but wide enough for the passage of horse-drawn carriages and carts.

With its 12-pinnacled tower, St Ive is unique as a parish church in Cornwall. Over the southern entrance porch in a vertical profile, is a sundial dated 1695 with a Latin motto, Quotidie Morior (I die day by day).

The interior of the church contains one modern feature – a small figure of a woman helping three children. It was presented to the church in honour of Emily's memory and sculpted by Jean Doyle of Cape Town, South Africa.

Designed and commissioned by Roy L Allen, author of That Englishwoman, the plinth bears the following engraving:

Dedicated to the Spirit and Devotion of Emily Hobhouse. Daughter of Rev Reginald Hobhouse. She saved children during the Anglo Boer War in South Africa and in World War I. She also pioneered Social Work and Temperance in America and Mexico. She is revered in South Africa where her ashes rest in the Women's Memorial Bloemfontein. Presented by Guide Caroline and Cub Sean Allen, on behalf of the 7th Green and Sea Point Group and Ellerton Primary School, Capetown, South Africa. 1991.

In 1923, The Declaration On The Rights Of The Child, proposed by Eglantyne Jebb, was adopted by The League Of Nations.

The present United Nations Charter adopted these "rights", declaring: "Men and women of all nations recognising that Mankind owes to the child the best that it has to give, declare and accept it as their duty that, beyond and above all considerations of race, nationality, or creed, the child that is hungry must be fed, the child that is sick must be nursed. The orphan and the waif must be sheltered and succoured. The child must be the first to receive relief in times of distress."

Emily Hobhouse was one of the first humanitarian workers to bring about the aims of the Charter, often in the face of derisory comments and punishments.

Her famous ancestor, the celebrated Bishop Trelawny, inspired the well-known Cornish anthem "And shall Trelawny die, then 20,000 Cornishmen shall know the reason why".

There is no reason why the international deeds of Emily Hobhouse should not be remembered and celebrated with pride, too.

This great woman fully deserves to be recognised by the British nation for her humanitarian achievements for the benefit of mankind.

EMILY'S HOUSE AT PORTHMINSTER, ST. IVES, CORNWALL

Originally purchased for her through subscriptions from
grateful South Africans.
This house currently forms part of the prestigious
Porthminster Hotel.

Appendix I

A N ARTICLE, printed in the Cornish Magazine in 1899 and reproduced here in its entirety, shows the depth of Emily's insight and social conscience – on this occasion, on the plight of the Cornish miners who left to dig for America. The article is in Emily's own words.

CORNISH MEN AND THE FAR WEST

EMIGRATION has forged strong links between Cornwall and America. Cornishmen are scattered more or less throughout the length and breadth of that continent, but probably the largest number congregate round the iron and copper mines of the North-western States. Some account of the mining districts in those States is here given, with a sketch of the conditions under which a miner lives in pioneer mining towns.

In most cases young men leave home, having seen nothing of their native country beyond a few villages and the neighbouring market town, and after twelve or fifteen days' incessant travel, find themselves in a new world, quite remote from anything their imagination could have pictured. People who have never been in any but old countries would be surprised at the newness of a new one; they do not realise how much they have been owing all their lives to the softening hand of time. This newness is in itself a shock, and if the Celtic nature were not extremely adaptable, the impulse to turn round and come back again would surely be acted upon. Many things so dear and familiar as to have seemed essential to life are absent there. An emigrating youth is hardly prepared for such a change. He leaves home vaguely feeling that in America "things are different", but how different, or in what way the differences will affect him, he rarely knows. Giddy with unwonted travel, he opens his eyes upon this land where all things are new: so new, in the pioneer towns now to be described, so recently carved out of the vast backwoods of Michegan, Minnesota, Wisconsin, and kindred States, that perhaps only six, four, or two years before all was impenetrable forest. In this forest a clearing has been made, possibly by a "wind-row", which in a few minutes leaves every tree in its path prostrate, like a field of grass when the mowers have passed; or the mighty pines have fallen by the axe; but generally fire has played its part, and the new town rises amid the headless, blackened trunks of burnt trees standing up on all sides in perpetual mourning for their past magnificence.

Across and across this clearing roads are marked out, chessboard-wise, and straight as rule and line can make them. Being mostly too new to walk upon, they are rapidly flanked with wooden sidewalks, to make locomotion possible. So from square to square one moves, feeling the while like a chessman.

Each side of the road the ground is staked out into lots, and on the lots up spring the wooden houses. These are so built that they can if preferred be easily moved to a more

196

suitable lot, or even to a neighbouring settlement. The first buildings of any size are mainly "saloons". The newer the town the larger the proportion of saloons. Indeed, a road and a saloon is often the nucleus of a town. As the town "booms", people pour in, and in two or three weeks large boarding-houses spring up. Then the State rears its school, and in course of time a church appears upon the scene, probably Presbyterian or Methodist Episcopal. Whatever denomination they may belong to, these churches are sure to be all wooden structures, equally appalling from an artistic point of view, so hideous that in comparison many a Cornish meeting house is an architectural triumph.

This infant community is not long content to remain a village. Far from it. In a year or so (obtaining powers from the State) it becomes a full-blown city, with mayor, town council, police force, fire brigade, and all the paraphernalia of a municipality, is lit by electric light, and publishes two or three daily papers. Those same papers are of the worst possible tone, and quite full of ignorance. Competition is very keen, and they vie with each other in recording the slightest actions of most insignificant private people with greater minuteness than if they were English royalties.

The fire brigade is necessary, for fires are very frequent. Indeed, they are the chief excitement such places afford, and all the city runs together at the alarm. If fire has started in a house it can generally be got under, but a forest fire is a different matter. A fire-wave which, issuing from the forest, rolls over the wood-built town consumes it in a few minutes, the hot breath of the fire doing more injury than the actual flames. The best thing to do in such a danger is to go and stand in the lake till the wave has passed. Fortunately, lakes are abundant, so this is possible. When all is over, and the heat abated sufficiently to enable the inhabitants to leave the water, they return to find every possession burned or melted, and every bit of shallower water licked dry; the whole process occupying less than half an hour.

There is no beauty in these settlements. Ugliness obtrudes itself upon you at every turn. Beauty can only be found by going outside and beyond the town clearing. There, standing on some elevated spot, those who have eyes to see can see it in the wide sweep of hill and plain, mantled as far as eye can reach in the dark green of primeval forest, in the blue of the countless lakes, in the scarlet and gold livery donned every autumn by maples and birches, in the glistening snows of the cruel winter, and the almost nightly glory of the Northern lights. But the average miner is blind to these things. To him the bush is only attractive as a place for hunting and shooting, where game-keepers are not known.

To this raw life, all unprepared, comes many a Cornish lad. He has left behind him cosy Cornish cottages of stone and slate, the bright flower-patch in front, the useful vegetable strip at the back. Old churches have always been in the background of his life, with hoary lichen-covered towers, the centre and pride of as many clustering villages; hamlets grouped about their substantial chapels; cheerful inns, where motherly landladies serve their customers, often talking to them the while "for their good"; but out West he may look for such things in vain. Green fields and grassy lawns, good English roads and countless lanes, squires' places dotted about, making still lovelier spots in a lovely land, these, too, are wholly absent.

Gone, moreover, are the men and women whose characters or positions lads have been brought up to revere; gone are feasts and revels and teas, and suchlike simple pleasurable days; gone the shorter working hours, the leisurely Sunday, the occasional half-holidays – in a word gone everything that goes to make up the life and spirit of English village homes. Instead of the familiar companionship of the villagers, strange faces and tongues surround him. The mines that attract him draw also swarms of men of other nations and languages. Norwegians and Swedes and Finlanders, Danes, Poles and Germans, Austrians and Bohemians, French and Italians, Scotch, Irish and Canadians, these with a sprinkling of negroes and the true-born Americans go to make up the population of every pioneer mining town. Nor must the Chinaman be omitted from the list. Who else would provide cheap restaurants and do the best and finest washing?

Yet, though all Europe is represented in every mining range, the Cornishman has the best chance. He is the skilled miner, as much at home underground as he is "to grass". He understands hard-rock mining, and none can rival him unless, perhaps, it is the Swede. Not long since, when Chicago was being tunnelled for some drainage works, the authorities had to telegraph to the north for

Cornish miners to come and deal with the mining of the hard rock.

Finns, Italians, and others do the inferior parts of the work and the soft ore mining. Thus Cornishmen get work without difficulty on account of their skill, and if sober soon rise to the most responsible and remunerative positions in the mines. The majority of superintendents, captains and "bosses" of every degree are from Cornwall. Soon they are inhabiting the smart roomy houses built for them by the companies in the precincts of the mines, and are in receipt of incomes which enable them to retire comfortably when age makes work a burden. Many such there are, and as far as material comfort goes their careers are successful. One such, a superintendent, whose thirty years in the States had left him every inch a Cornishman, said he owed his prosperity to one simple rule. He early determined, work permitting, always to be in bed by 11pm, and this little rule of life, never swerved from, had saved him. However, he had the further advantage of a Cornishwoman for his wife. She, after eleven years' working the fields as farm-girl in a lonely Cornish parish, had emigrated to seek her fortune, and fell easily into her new position as a smart lady, drove in her carriage or her sleigh according to season, and made her husband thoroughly happy. In the house of such a man comfort reigns and bids defiance to the dismal world without. His table is loaded with American delicacies, but saffron cake and pasties still find a place, and spite of an unwilling climate Cornish cream adds the crowning touch to his meal. Such well-placed and successful men rarely go home again to live. They have thrown in their lives with the American people, take interest in public affairs, have considerable influence in their neighbourhoods, and often control the politics of their town. Some of them take a labouring oar in the task of building up the life of newly settled communities.

But there is the other side of the picture, and it is a dark one – the fate of the majority, who fall down and worship before the drink idol which the saloon-keeper sets up. It is exceedingly hard for them not to do this, and it is not possible for mothers, wives, and sweethearts sitting in sheltered Cornish homes to judge them justly.

Nursed, may be, in a Band of Hope, grafted later into some blue ribbon or temperance society, the young man goes away sure of himself, not realising that Cornwall (shown by statistics to be about the soberest of English counties) presents comparatively no temptation to drink. To make the matter plain, imagine what it would be like if the conditions of towns such as are now being described were introduced into Cornwall. Take a village with the population of Roche or St Cleer, and let some thirty or forty saloons spring up where one or two old-fashioned inns now stand. And let it be remembered that the saloonkeepers themselves would be a serious importation, being of a type mercifully rare in English villages. Or take towns like Liskeard or St Austell, full of homelike quiet beauty, tear down every good and noble building, string saloons on either side of the principal streets, sprinkle them thickly in back streets and at every prominent corner, strew drunkards in varying stages of intoxication on the sidewalks, provide inside liquor so adulterated that a man wants to drink and drink again, surround him with foreigners of a lower type than himself, take away all amusements except those in which the saloonkeeper is head and chief, recollect there is no precedent for anything, and finally sweep away all public opinion save that which looks on drunkenness as an amiable weakness. How would the number of drunken cases compare with the present figures? Add to this a climate of great extremes, very exciting and so dry that lips and throat are parched – a contrast indeed to the temperate and moist Cornish atmosphere – and last, but not least, the dis-comfort of having no home but a boarding-house, where day and night a ceaseless struggle is carried on by loud-voiced women to get meals on the table for the various shifts, or, if that is too costly, a shanty on the outskirts of the town. Here the man must "batch" either alone or with a mate. He can build his shack himself with a few upright poles and cover it with black tar paper to keep out the cold. After eleven hours at the mine he returns to cook his own dismal meal, and if he has time on Sundays he must wash and bake. But it not being good for man to live alone, he grows careless and ruffianly, and want of companionship drives him to the saloon. Nevertheless there are cases where these "shacks" are models of cleanliness and neatness, inhabited by men who prefer quietness to the rough com-pany of the boarding-house.

When a man arrives from the old country the saloon-keeper is on the watch for the few pounds he may have in his pocket. One man said he landed with £50 (his father had some means:), and at the week's end had 2s 6d left. He hastened to explain he had not drunk the whole value himself, but the treating system prevails extensively and empties pockets rapidly. He had continued to drink very hard for thirty years, but was none the less a good sort of man and JP for his city. The saloons vary from the better class, which have a billiard board and are patronised by professional men, politicians, and the like, through all stages to the lowest, which are the resort of Italians, Irish, Austrians, etc. Generally each nationality has its saloon, but often, too, the saloon-keeper is an apt man, who learns half a dozen languages in order to make various customers feel at home. He baits his premises with free lunches, hot suppers, free samples, and all manner of devices to allure, and the green youth from the old country speedily falls prey. Then when pay-day comes the saloon-keeper puts forth every effort to reap what he has not sown. Spree and recovery take a man a week, and money which should have been travelling back to Cornwall or paying the "board-missis" is safe in the saloon till. He has treated and been treated, he is in debt to the saloon, in debt for his board, and having nothing to send home is ashamed to write. So it goes on, and when there is a wife and family at home the suffering for them is terrible. Yet their suffering can hardly be as great as that of the wretch who drags on through a weary life, always with the consciousness, however dimmed, of unfulfilled duty, bound hand and foot by drink and debt, with just grace enough left to be ashamed and shrink from the sight of anyone fresh from the old country. Yet, even here, harsh judgment must be tempered by the thought that some minds are so constituted that a completely new set of scenes and impressions affect them so strongly as almost to obliterate the past. Even the names of those known from youth upwards can be wiped from the memory in a few months by the obliterating power of a complete change.

So dim and dream-like and shadowy becomes the old life to many of these untutored minds. Correspondence across the hemispheres is but a sorry link at best. How much more so when writing is not, and cannot be, the vehicle of thought, and the man when he has written to his wife is as much alone as ever so far as interchange of thought goes. When, as often, he is too illiterate even to scrawl his own few empty sentences, then an acquaintance must be called in to act as medium between man and wife. All these things lead to a darker side, which cannot be touched on here. Cost what it may (and it can be cheaply done), wives should emigrate with their husbands – families should keep together. In the West Country the family can live far more cheaply in proportion than the single man, and it is the only chance of real happiness and comfort. The unmarried who emigrate find it hard to marry there, for women are very scarce. Besides, the Cornishman thinks the American girl too much of a fine lady, with her novel and her rocking-chair, and she thinks "Cousin Jack" a curiosity, with his quaint dialect and the old world notions that hang about him. Sometimes he weds a Swede or Norwegian, fair of face and thrifty in house matters;

more often he loafs about year after year without the steadying influence that marriage would bring him.

It is difficult to bring any abiding influence to bear upon these frontier towns because of the fluctuating character of their inhabitants. Here today and gone tomorrow! To stay three months is to be an old resident. Both houses and people move about in a way that would be the despair of a district visitor, and a labour leader finds it equally difficult to organise trades unions.

Disturbance amongst Eastern capitalists frequently causes the mines to close down suddenly, completely paralysing the business of places which depend solely on them for the influx of money. In such intervals of enforced idleness the whole energetic part of the population moves off, tramping or "car-jumping" if cash is short, and the empty town adds desolation to its other charms. Taking one part with another, there is always in America a large restless, fluctuating population, ready to rush to any new place that may be "booming". Why not? They have no particular motive to keep them in the one spot, nothing to bind them to a special place, no link with anybody or anything, no roots in the past such as may influence an Englishman to remain where his name can be traced back in the church registers, and his fathers have mined the ground before him. But in spite of the crudeness which is the prevailing note of the Far West, romance reigns there, poetry too goes pioneering, in the wake of human life, and dark and sorry spots are illumined by the brilliance of noble deeds.

If asked why they left their pretty Cornish homes for this

rough life, extreme in climate, where equal comforts can only be procured at double cost, the miner's answer is always the same, though couched in many forms. It is dimly felt by some, clearly seen by others, that, notwithstanding hardship and discomfort, before them lies development, progress, possibility. Many old world conventionalities have dropped off like worn-out garments; and the sense of freedom is exhilarating. In a word they have tasted life, in comparison with which the cramped existence of a Cornish village is stagnation.

Those Western States embody all that is incidental to youth. They are raw, ignorant, hot-headed, but equally they are instinct with life and hope and energy. Repeatedly repulsed they never despair, but start afresh with undying pluck and determination. One would be insensible, indeed, to live in such an atmosphere and not be conscious of the throb of youthful heart-beat, and this it is which charms and attracts. Population pours in, towns spring up, cities develop, new communities are building up a great new country, greater than in the old in width and scope and material resource, and Cornishmen are helping to do this.

If they are to do their share of the work well and nobly, they should receive the necessary training before they leave their native village. What they need is character, firm, well-developed character, based upon a few deep, broad principles of life such as can be adapted and re-adapted to meet every circumstance, and such as will stand the strain of all demands made upon them by the changes and chances of the unknown. EMILY HOBHOUSE

Appendix II

EMILY Hobhouse grew up in Cornwall and the area was clearly precious to her. The following are a few notes on some of the parts of Cornwall that meant something to Emily and which a reader can still share her pleasure in today.

Caradon Hill was a great attraction to the adventurous young Emily. From its summit on a clear day, a beautiful panorama of expansive views presents itself.

To the east in the distance can be seen the dramatic land mass of Dartmoor in Devon. Caradon itself is within the confines of the intriguing and mysterious Bodmin Moor, which adds to the reputation that Cornwall, land of the saints, is a place of history, mystery and legend.

Further attractions to Emily on this moor, in close proximity, included a monolith known as the Cheeswring, a Neolithic pile of unusually-stacked granite stones, and a collection of standing stones called The Hurlers. Legend has it that the huge stones represented players in the Cornish game of Hurling. The players were turned into stone for playing this game on the Sabbath.

Yet another of Emily's favourite walks was to the village of Quethiock two miles south of St Ive. The main attraction in Quethiock is the 13th Century Church of St Hugh.

The parson of this parish church, the Reverend William Willimott (1878-1888), had similar developmental ideas to his colleague, Emily's father Reginald Hobhouse.

Willimott, with his own hands, put a great deal of effort into the restoration of this fine church. One intriguing historical artefact in the grounds of St Hugh is the granite wheel-headed cross which had stood for 800 years until it was torn down and smashed during the Reformation. In 1881 the cross was restored, its three broken pieces re-united. It was re-erected near the baptismal well.

Almost the same distance to the east of Emily's family home was another ancient site, the virtually conical hill of Cadson Bury. On its brow, encircled by a tremendous earthwork, stands the remains of an Iron Age hill fort.

Beneath Cadson Bury and enveloped in a scene of rustic beauty, there stands an angularly recessed stone bridge. New Bridge, as it is called, forms part of the A390 roadway, and crosses over the meandering river Lynher. On the hill fort side of this river are scenic trails that intrigued Emily with their peacefulness.

BIBLIOGRAPHY

Amery, L S – The Times History Of The War In South Africa Vols 1-6 (William Clowes & Sons, London)

Armstrong, M – Trelawny (Macmillan & Co, N York, 1940)

Balme, J Hobhouse – To Love One's Enemies (Hobhouse Trust, 1994)

Barthorp, Michael – The Anglo Boer War (Blandford Press, 1987)

Bayley, Christopher – Atlas Of The British Empire (Facts On File, 1989)

Belchem, John – Popular Radicalism In 19th Century Britain (Macmillan, 1996)

Benbow, Colin – Boer Prisoners of War in Bermuda (Island Press, 1994)

Birrell, Augustine – Things Past Redress (Faber, 1987)

Bishop, George – A Parish Album Of St Ive (Columbian Press, 1988)

Brett, S R – British History 1783-1939 (Butler & Tanner, 1934)

Cook, J and **Entwistle, T R** – Factbook Of British History (Aurora Enterprises, 1984)

Costain, A J – Lord Roberts, His Life Story (Epworth Press, 1925)

EI Madhi, Mandour – A Short History Of The Sudan (Oxford University Press, 1965)

Feiling, Keith – A History Of England (Book Club Associates, 1950)

Fisher, John – That Miss Hobhouse (Secker & Warburg, 1971)

Green, John R – Short History Of The English People (Macmillan, 1891)

Grass, John – Rudyard Kipling (Weidenfield & Nicolson, 1972)

Grant, R G – Winston Churchill Biography (Bison Books, 1989)

Gunter, John – Inside Africa (Hamish Hamilton, 1987)

Hobhouse, Emily – Cornishmen And The Far West (Cornish Magazine, 1899)

Hobhouse, Emily – The Brunt of the War and Where It Fell (Methuen, 1902)

Hoyland, John S – Modern European History (G Bell & Sons, 1924)

Jeal, Tim – Livingstone (Chaucer Press, 1973)

Kiley, Dennis – South Africa (B T Batsford, 1976)

Kruger, Rayne – Goodbye Dolly Gray (Pan Books, 1974)

Lamb, David – The Africans (Vintage Books, 1984)

Legrande, Jacques – Chronicle Of The 20th Century (Longman Chronicle, 1988)

Longford, Elizabeth – Victoria R I (Weidenfeld & Nicolson, 1964)

Mackenzie, John M – Imperialism & Popular Culture (Manchester University Press, 1986)

Mandela, Nelson – Long Walk To Freedom (Abacus, 1994)

Millin, Sarah G – Rhodes (Chatto & Windus, 1937)

Moorehead, Alan – The White Nile (Penguin, 1933)

Moynahan, Brian – The British Century (Weidenfeld & Nicolson, 1997)

Moberly Bell, E – Flora Shaw, Lady Lugard DBE (Constable, 1946)

Nicolson, Colin – The Making Of Africa (Wayland Publishers, 1973)

Paton, Alan – Journey Continued (Oxford University Press, 1988)

Pemberton, W B – Battles Of The Boer War (Pan Books, 1964)

Raynes, J R – The Pageant Of England 1900-20 (Swathmore Press, 1920)

Roberts, Brian – Those Bloody Women (John Murray, 1991)

Sacks, J – The Politics Of Hope (Mackays Chatham, 1997)

Slater, Francis C – New Century Book Of S African Verse (Longmans Green, 1945)

Smuts, J C – Jan Christian Smuts (Cassell & Co, 1952)

Spender, J A – Gt Britain Empire & Commonwealth (Cassell & Co, 1935)

Stacey, M and **Price, M** – Women, Power & Politics (Tavistock Publications, 1981)

Thomas, Antony – Rhodes, The Race for Africa (Penguin BBC Books, 1996)

Thomas, David – Europe Since Napoleon (Penguin Books, 1957)

Trevelyan, G M – British History In The 19th Century (Longmans Green, 1922)

Trevelyan, G M – English Social History (Longmans Green, 1944)

Weech, W N – History Of The World (Odhams Press, 1942)

Welsh, F – A History Of South Africa (Harper Collins, 1998)

White, R J – A Short History Of England (Cambridge University Press, 1967)

Winter, J M – World War I, Vol 2 (Hamlyn, 1988)

REFERENCES

Abbreviations:

      T.H.W.S.A.   Times History of the War in South Africa

      E.H.   Emily Hobhouse

Chapt. 1 **The Heyday of Imperialism.**

      Queen Victoria.   Victoria R.I.   Longford E

      Advertisement   Cornish Times   1900

Chapt. 2 **The Hobhouse Family in St. Ive.**

      Bishop Trelawny   History of English People   1891

Chapt. 3 **A New Life**

      Chronological Dates.   Chronicle of 20th Century

      That Miss Hobhouse.   Fisher J. op.cit.

      Hobhouse Family History.   To Love One's Enemies

                                   Balme. J.H. et. al.

      British Working Conditions, English Social History,

                                     Trevelyan. G.M.

      S. Africa Early History.   British History   Brett. S.R.

      London Missionary Society. History of England   Feiling. K.

      Chamberlain, Milner & Rhodes Modern European History,

                                       Hoyland. J.S.

Chapt. 4 **War Inevitable**

      Buller Criticism.   Goodbye Dolly Gray.   Kruger. R.

      Hostility of Norma Roberts. Those Bloody Women. Roberts. B.

      Churchill Criticism.   Winston Churchill.   Grant. R.G.

      Robert's Knighthood   Goodbye Dolly Gray.   Kruger. R.

      Relief for Camp Internees   To Love One's Enemies

                                     Balme. J.H. et. al.

Chapt. 5 **The Political Scene**

      Daily Chronicle Letter   Rt. Hon. H.Hobhouse Sept. 1899

      Annexation Proclamation   T.H.W.S.A. Vol.3   Amery. L.S.

      Martial Law   T.H.W.S.A. Vol.6   Amery. L.S.

Chapt. 6 Farm Burning
Hague Convention Articles   The Brunt of the War   Sept 1899
Anarchist Plot   T.H.W.S.A. Vol.6   Amery. L.S.

Chapt. 7 Shouted Down
Public Meeting Report   Cornish Times   1900

Chapt. 8 A Visit To The South African Camps
Ref. Quakers   Pears Encyc. 86th Edn.   Cook. C.
E.H. Camp Experiences   To Love One's Enemies
                                                      Balme. J.H.
That Bloody Woman Reference   Goodbye Dolly Gray.   Kruger. R.

Chapt. 9 Return To The U.K.
E.H. Discussion with Milner   Those Bloody Women. Roberts. B.
Lady Maxwell's Appeal   N.York Herald Tribune.   1901
House of Commons Debate   Hansard 4th Series   X.C.V.
National Reform Union Banquet The Times   15. 6. 1901
E.H. Lampooned   Punch Magazine   3. 7. 1901
E.H. Praised   Bristol Mercury   10. 7. 1901

Chapt. 10 The Committee of Lady Visitors.
Letter F/Marshall Chamberlain Manchester Guardian   5. 8. 1901
Ladies Commission Report   To Love One's Enemies
                                                      Balme. J.H.
Buller Relieved of Command   Chronicle of 20th Century
                                                      Mercer. D.
Camp Death Rates   Chronicle of 20th Century
                                                      Mercer. D.

Chapt. 11 Deported
Martial Law   T.H.W.S.A. Vol.6   Amery. L.S.
E.H. Deportation   To Love One's Enemies
                                                      Balme. J.H.
E.H. Further Praise For   Daily News   25. 11. 1901

Chapt. 12 The Prisoner Returns
Legal Proceedings   To Love One's Enemies
                                                      Balme. J.H.

Chapt. 13 The Suffering Of The Blacks
    Letters   The Brunt of the War   E.H. 1902
    Black Camp Inmates   The Times   25. 7. 1901

Chapt. 14 Peace In South Africa
    Vereeniging Settlement   T.H.W.S.A. Vol.6   Amery. L.S.
    E.H. Visit & Experiences That Miss Hobhouse
                                      Fisher. J. et. al.
    E.H. Apology   Jan Christian Smuts
                                     Smuts. J.C. (son).

Chapt. 15 Dear Mr Gandhi.
    Gandhi's S. African Crusade Jan Christian Smuts
                                     Smuts. J.C. (son).

Chapt. 16 World War On
    Karl Liebnecht Demonstration World War 1, Vol.2.   Hamlyn.
    E.H. Germany Visit   That Miss Hobhouse   Fisher. J.
    Edith Cavell   Encyc. Britt.
    Progress of W.W. One   Chronicle of 20th Century
                                       Longman

Chapt. 17 The Aftermath of War
                              Letter from Save The Children
                              General Secretary   19 .03. 01

Chapt. 18 Physical Deterioration
    Death & Burial of E.H.   To Love One's Enemies
                                      Balme. J.H. et al.
    Smuts Obituary Address   Bloemfontein Friend
                                      28. 10. 1926
    Poem. Now With This Love   Webster. M.M.

Chapt. 19 The Influence Of The Times
    Moberly Bell & Flora Shaw Biography of Flora Shaw
                                      Bell. E.M.

Epilogue
    The Author   Beer. F.H.

Appendices
    1. Cornishmen and the Far West Cornish Magazine 1899   E.H.
    2. E.H. Local Environment   Local Comments   Beer. F.H.